Interpersonal Communication Workshop

Second Edition

Sharon D. Downey

California State University, Long Beach

BURGESS INTERNATIONAL GROUP INC
Burgess Publishing

Copyright © 1994, 1993 by BURGESS INTERNATIONAL GROUP, Inc.,
Burgess Publishing Division
ISBN 0-8087-4487-9

Printed in the United States of America.
J I H G F

Address orders to:

BURGESS INTERNATIONAL GROUP, Inc.
7110 Ohms Lane
Edina, Minnesota 55439-2143
Telephone 612/831-1344
EasyLink 629-106-44
Fax 612/831-3167

Burgess Publishing
A Division of BURGESS INTERNATIONAL GROUP, Inc.

PURPOSE OF THE WORKBOOK

Oriented exclusively to building communication skills, this _Interpersonal Communication Workbook_ is designed to supplement a conceptually-based interpersonal communication textbook. It is presumed that students will gain theoretical knowledge of interpersonal communication via such a textbook, and through lectures, selected readings, written assignments, and examinations. The workbook, then, extends those theoretical principles by offering students the opportunity to develop and improve their communication skills for the purpose of strengthening the quality and satisfaction of their interpersonal relationships.

What follows is a collection of handouts, exercises, simulations, and assignments to facilitate development of a variety of communication skills. Some activities require that students assess their own communication patterns; some ask that they observe others' communicative dynamics; some request that they identify the recurrent communicative patterns that emerge in their most important relationships; some activities offer them the opportunity to try out new behaviors and gauge their effectiveness or ineffectiveness; and some activities compel them to test the efficacy of communication theories.

Perfect communication in interpersonal relationships is impossible. But more constructive and affirming communication is possible if students learn to accept the view that their communication choices are determined by the knowledge they possess. Consequently, enhancing knowledge increases choices. Such is the goal of this workbook.

TABLE OF CONTENTS

THE NATURE OF COMMUNICATION

Introduction to Communication

Attitudes toward Communication

Verbal Communication

Nonverbal Communication

THE PERFECT MATCH

Goal: The purpose of this exercise is to allow you to become acquainted with each other. At the same time, the activity introduces you to the interpersonal perspective of the course.

Instructions: You are required to find a person in class who matches the description of each item contained in the list of statements below. An individual's name should <u>not</u> be placed with more than one item. Begin your search; the exercise is complete when you have filled in the blanks for all of the statements.

_____   A person who has blue eyes.

_____   A person who is wearing tennis shoes.

_____   A person who is taller than you.

_____   A person of the opposite sex.

_____   A person who is wearing eye glasses.

_____   A person who has read a book.

_____   A person who was born in a different town.

_____   A person who likes spaghetti.

_____   A person who likes to sleep late in the morning.

_____   A person who has studied a foreign language.

_____   A person who has the same color hair as yourself.

_____   A person who has the same major.

_____   A person who cannot swim.

_____   A person who plays a musical instrument.

_____   A person who wears clean underwear.

Discussion: Are there any parallels between this exercise and your impressions in real-life situations like fraternity and sorority rush parties, cocktail parties, beginning of the school year gatherings, etc? Your assessment should include the topics discussed, the depth of the conversation, the nonverbal behavior, the stylistic language, the hesitancy and/or ease of interaction.

Source: Mark L. Knapp, and Anita L. Vangelisti. <u>Interpersonal Communication and Human Relationships</u>, 2nd. ed. (Instructor's Manual). Boston: Allyn & Bacon, 1992, pp. 7-8.

BRUSH WITH GREATNESS

Goal: This exercise is designed to create a non-threatening, positive class atmosphere and to introduce class members to each other.

Instructions: This activity is inspired by the television show "Late Night with David Letterman." Letterman occasionally runs a segment titled "Brush with Greatness." Audience members describe incidents about famous people with whom they have had contact.

You should prepare a brief story to relate to the class about meeting celebrities, attending well known events, or visiting famous places. Examples may include contacts ranging from fishing with John Wayne to meeting the Emperor of Japan.

Discussion: Discussion should surround whether this form of casual, personal information is easier to relay than other forms of introduction, and whether such forms of identification create a more relaxed class atmosphere.

Source: Sean Raftis. "Brush with Greatness." The Speech Teacher, 5 (1991): 5.

WHAT CONSTITUTES COMMUNICATION?

Goal: To identify instances where communication has and has not occurred.

Instructions: For each of the following scenarios, answer "YES" if you believe communication has occurred and "NO" if you believe no communication has occurred. Next to the example, write one reason for why you chose the answer you did.

<u>Yes</u>   <u>No</u>

___   ___   1. You are getting on a public bus heading toward your home. As you get on, you notice a grubby looking weirdo puffing on a cigarette butt. You decide to sit in a different seat near the driver.

___   ___   2. Madge Nadworthy pulls two slices of by-now-charcoal toast from the toaster. Her husband, Waldo, goes right on reading the paper as the smell fills the kitchen.

___   ___   3. Armondo is a continental Italian-lover type. Every Friday night he frequents a certain hip disco club. Once there, he invariably meets some would-be starlet, promises her a motion picture contract, plies her with martinis, and whisks her back to his apartment for the coup de gras.

___   ___   4. You are having dinner with your family. In order to add some excitement to the Hamburger Helper, you bring up some eventful topics, including the President's unwillingness to raise taxes, the status of women in the United States, and the price of textbooks. No one seems interested.

___   ___   5. Miranda Lardwell's English professor assigns her to analyze Byron's <u>Marin Faliero II</u>. Miranda is unable to make heads or tails out of the poem and decided that it's a piece of junk.

___   ___   6. Bennie Lackluster has been dying to get a date with Loretta Whizbang for weeks. He finally obtains her phone number from a mutual friend and calls her that evening. A previous engagement prevents Loretta from going out that night. Bennie wonders if he should try again next week or just forget it.

___   ___   7. Mary needs a new yellow t-shirt. After looking at those on the rack, she ignores the ones proclaiming "Foxy Lady," "Hot Stuff," and "It's My Body . . . but I Share." She chooses a plain yellow t-shirt with no message on it and wears it out of the store.

Discussion: Can you identify the "message" in each of the above examples? Is communication sender- or receiver-oriented? What component determined your decision to answer "YES" to any of the above examples?

4

MODEL OF COMMUNICATION EXERCISE

Goal: To illustrate various elements of the model of communication. Particular importance is place on feedback in order to facilitate more effective and efficient communication.

Instructions:

1.   Pair off into groups of two. Arrange your chairs so that you are seated back-to-back with one another. In other words, you must be positioned so that you cannot see each other.

2.   Your instructor will give one of you a drawing or figure (probably a geometric design). Whichever one of you possess the drawing is the sender. Your partner is the receiver. Your task is to verbally describe to your partner this drawing; your partner will reproduce this drawing based solely on your instructions. However, during this part of the exercise, the receiver cannot talk, look at, ask questions, provide feedback, or in any way communicate with the sender. This is the "no feedback" condition. You may look at each other's drawing after the sender has completed giving instructions.

3.   After the first round is completed, the sender and receiver will reverse roles. The instructor will provide you with a new drawing or figure. Your task is the same: the sender must tell the receiver how to reproduce the drawing or figure exactly. This time, however, the sender and receiver can talk to one another. Feel free to ask questions, request clarification, repeat an instruction. You still cannot look at each other's drawing until you have completed the exercise. This is the "feedback" portion of the activity.

Discussion: Discussion should surround what communication problems occurred without feedback (encoding and decoding, for examples); what problems are solved with the use of feedback (if any); what new problems emerged with feedback (i.e., assuming); how participants feel about communicating without feedback; and what skills could be adopted to better insure the efficient and effective transmission of messages and shared meaning.

STATEMENTS ABOUT COMMUNICATION

Goal: To identify your views about the nature of communication.

Instructions: Several statements are listed below. To the left of each statement are the letters A and D. Circle A if you tend to agree with the statement or think it is essentially correct; circle D if you disagree with the statement or think it is essentially incorrect. Complete these statements individually first. Then form groups of 4-6 persons and arrive at a consensus as a group. The group should be prepared to justify why it agreed or disagreed with each statement.

Individual	Group		
A D	A D	1.	Communication occurs when one person sends a message to another person.
A D	A D	2.	Communication occurs when a receiver of a message assigns meaning to it.
A D	A D	3.	The more people have in common, the better they can communicate.
A D	A D	4.	Whenever there is a breakdown in communication, it is usually the fault of the message sender.
A D	A D	5.	The actual sending of the message is the most important event in communication.
A D	A D	6.	A conversation between two people takes place in discrete segments; that is, one person sends a message and the other person receives the message. Then the process is reversed as the other person sends and the first person receives.
A D	A D	7.	Feedback is information a person gets by scanning the environment to see how well her or his actions are adapting to the context.
A D	A D	8.	Feedback is necessary to increase the accuracy of communication.
A D	A D	9.	Most of the world's problems are communication problems that could be solved if people simply understood each other better.
A D	A D	10.	Communication between two people is a relatively simple matter.
A D	A D	11.	Most communication transactions are quite simple once you understand what is going on.

Discussion: What are the most important variables or components of any communication exchange? What qualifies as an instance of communication? What qualifies as a noncommunication?

6

INTERPERSONAL COMMUNICATION
QUESTIONNAIRE

Goal: To identify your strengths and weaknesses in communicating in interpersonal relationships.

Instructions: Answer the statements below using the following scale: 5 = strongly agree; 4 = agree; 3 = neither agree nor disagree; 2 = disagree; 1 = strongly disagree.

_____ 1. I say what I mean and mean what I say.

_____ 2. I ask for clarification when I don't understand what someone has said to me.

_____ 3. I don't let others put words in my mouth.

_____ 4. I have no problems expressing myself in conversations.

_____ 5. I don't get tongue-tied in interactions with others.

_____ 6. In conversations, I try to talk about things that are interesting to both the other and me.

_____ 7. I let others know when I disagree with them.

_____ 8. I try to understand others by putting myself in their shoes.

_____ 9. The other and I spend about equal time talking and listening.

_____ 10. I am aware of how I sound to others when I am talking.

_____ 11. I don't express my feelings if I think that they will unduly hurt another person.

_____ 12. I accept constructive criticism from others.

_____ 13. I don't have problems apologizing to others if I feel that I have hurt them.

_____ 14. I let others know when I am angry with them.

_____ 15. Verbal confrontations with others don't scare me.

_____ 16. I can accept compliments from others.

_____ 17. I trust others.

_____ 18. I like complimenting others.

_____ 19. I like it when others confide in me.

_____ 20. I can articulate my weaknesses to others.

_____ 21. I don't interrupt others.

_____ 22. I am a good listener.

_____ 23. I try to respond to what others both say and feel.

_____ 24. I am able to adjust quickly to others when I see how they react to what I am saying.

_____ 25. What I say is usually understood by others.

_____ **Total**

Interpreting Your Scores: The items above refer such interpersonal communication areas as listening, expressing feelings, emotions, understanding, and empathy. The higher your score (above 100), the more proficient and aware you are of your communication and its consequences; the lower your score (below 50), the more you need to attend to your communication practices and look at reactions to them. This should help you identify areas in which to improve.

IDEAL COMMUNICATION

Goal: This exercise is designed for you to identify communication patterns that do not meet your expectations for how you should act.

Instructions:

1. Place an "A" on the continuum that best reflects your perception of how you "actually" act in your everyday interactions with others. Then, on that same continuum, place an "I" to reflect your perception of how you would "ideally" like to behave.

2. After completing all of the scales, examine those areas in which the discrepancies from "A" to "I" are the greatest. These constitute areas for communication improvement. To facilitate skills development, write down an example of how you typically act on this dimension. Then, with the aid of group members in your class, identify concrete alternatives that you might be able to adopt in order to improve your communication in this area.

intellectual	__	__	__	__	__	nonintellectual
sad	__	__	__	__	__	happy
honest	__	__	__	__	__	dishonest
introverted	__	__	__	__	__	extroverted
friendly	__	__	__	__	__	unfriendly
tense	__	__	__	__	__	relaxed
flexible	__	__	__	__	__	inflexible
sympathetic	__	__	__	__	__	unsympathetic
active	__	__	__	__	__	passive
accepting	__	__	__	__	__	rejecting
humorous	__	__	__	__	__	serious
superficial	__	__	__	__	__	deep
strong	__	__	__	__	__	weak
optimistic	__	__	__	__	__	pessimistic

Discussion: Discuss discrepancies between your "real" and "ideal" communication patterns with class members. Do class members share many of these patterns? Try to account for why there is often a difference between our actual behavior and our desired or ideal behavior.

IDENTIFYING A COMMUNICATION
PROBLEM

Goal: This exercise is designed for you to identify one communication pattern with which you are dissatisfied and to try to improve that skill.

Instructions:

1. Think about some communication difficulty you have with other persons. Such difficulties may include an inability to be assertive; discomfort in initiating conversations with others; a tendency to avoid conflict situations; or a reluctance to self-disclose personal information.

2. Maintain a record of the opportunities that you had to use the skill during a one week period. At the end of this time, assess your performance. Consider some of the following in your assessment:

    a. Who were you interacting with when the skill was relevant? What was the other's communicative style?

    b. When did you use the skill performed most effectively? Least effectively?

    c. What other behaviors accompany this skill? Do they help or hinder this skill?

    d. How do you feel during the time you used this skill? Did your attitude contribute to the effective or ineffective use of this skill?

    e. What are the advantages and disadvantages of employing this skill?

Discussion: Write a one-page paper assessing your skill performance, and determine ways in which the skill may be improved, if warranted. Be prepared to discuss your experience in class.

INTERPERSONAL COMMUNICATION
SATISFACTION INVENTORY

Instructions: Your instructor has provided you with the opportunity to interact with a partner. The purpose of this questionnaire is to investigate your reactions to the conversation you just had. Please react to the following statements. Indicate the degree to which you agree or disagree that each statement describes this conversation. The 4 or middle position on the scale represents "undecided" or "neutral," then moves out from the center to "slight" agreement or disagreement, then to "moderate" agreement or disagreement, and finally to "strong" agreement or disagreement. Circle the number that best represents your feelings.

1.   The other person let me know that I was communicating effectively.
        Strongly Agree 7 6 5 4 3 2 1 Strongly Disagree

2.   Nothing was accomplished.
        Strongly Agree 1 2 3 4 5 6 7 Strongly Disagree

3.   I would like to have another conversation like this one.
        Strongly Agree 7 6 5 4 3 2 1 Strongly Disagree

4.   The other person genuinely wanted to get to know me.
        Strongly Agree 7 6 5 4 3 2 1 Strongly Disagree

5.   I was very dissatisfied with the conversation.
        Strongly Agree 1 2 3 4 5 6 7 Strongly Disagree

6.   I felt that during the conversation I was able to present myself as I wanted the other person to view me.
        Strongly Agree 7 6 5 4 3 2 1 Strongly Disagree

7.   I was very satisfied with the conversation.
        Strongly Agree 7 6 5 4 3 2 1 Strongly Disagree

8.   The other person expressed a lot of interest in what I had to say.
        Strongly Agree 7 6 5 4 3 2 1 Strongly Disagree

9.   I did not enjoy the conversation
        Strongly Agree 1 2 3 4 5 6 7 Strongly Disagree

10.   The other person did not provide support for what s/he was saying.
        Strongly Agree 1 2 3 4 5 6 7 Strongly Disagree

11.   I felt I could talk about anything with the other person.
        Strongly Agree 7 6 5 4 3 2 1 Strongly Disagree

12.   We each got to say what we wanted.
        Strongly Agree 7 6 5 4 3 2 1 Strongly Disagree

13.   I felt that we could laugh easily together.
        Strongly Agree 7 6 5 4 3 2 1 Strongly Disagree

14. The conversation flowed smoothly.
      Strongly Agree 7 6 5 4 3 2 1 Strongly Disagree

15. The other person frequently said things which added little to the conversation.
      Strongly Agree 1 2 3 4 5 6 7 Strongly Disagree

16. We talked about something I was not interested in.
      Strongly Agree 1 2 3 4 5 6 7 Strongly Disagree

Results: Add up all circled numbers _____.

         81 - 112 = high communication satisfaction
         48 - 80 = moderate communication satisfaction
         16 - 47 = low communication satisfaction

Discussion: Identify your most important criteria for evaluating a communication exchange as satisfactory or unsatisfactory. How much of this evaluation is dependent upon nonverbal factors? verbal factors? the outcome or productivity of the interaction?

Source: Michael L. Hecht. "The Conceptualization and Measurement of Interpersonal Communication Satisfaction." Human Communication Research, 4 (1978): 253-264.

MORE THAN MERE WORDS

Goal: To become aware of the view that language creates social reality, and to become more appreciative of the potentials of communication.

Instructions:

1. Take out <u>three</u> pieces of paper.

2. Take the first piece of paper and draw a picture of an ugly, creepy insect.

3. Take the second piece of paper and write the name of or draw a picture of your least favorite food.

4. Take the third piece of paper and write the name you use to address your mother.

5. Take the first piece of paper, put it on the floor and step repeatedly and enthusiastically on the bug.

6. Take the second piece of paper, put it on the floor and step on that horrid food.

7. Place the third piece of paper on the floor and stomp on it.

Discussion: Discussion should surround how words or symbols affect our reality, our behavior, and our perceptions of things. In other words, talk about the power of words and symbols. What made you hesitate to stomp on the word "mother?" Why was it so easy to do so with your detested bug or food? What is the relationship between words/symbols and the real things, people, and ideas they stand for?

Source: Edwin N. Rowley. "More Than Mere Words." Speech Communication Teacher, 7 (1992): 5.

MEANINGFUL RESPONSES

Goal: This exercise is designed to demonstrate the need to provide relevant feedback to others.

Instructions:

1. Form groups of 4 - 6 persons and, for approximately ten minutes, discuss each person's image of the ideal relational partner.

2. <u>No Feedback Condition</u>: For ten minutes, group members should respond to others' statements either by giving no feedback at all or by saying something completely unrelated to what the previous speaker said.

3. <u>Meaningful Responses</u>: Then, continue your discussion, but this time, each speaker's statement should be followed by a "paraphrase." This means to restate what the other person has said in your own words. Dialogue cannot continue until the speaker and the listener agree that they share the same meaning of the speaker's original statement. In other words, your paraphrase should match what the speaker meant in her/his statement.

Discussion: Discussion should surround what it felt like to talk and not receive appropriate feedback, and what it felt like to fail to repond meaningfully to another's remark. In addition, how did you feel after listening meaningfully to another's remarks, and how did you feel after being listened to in the same way? How often do we fail to listen and respond appropriately to another? How useful is the communication skill of paraphrasing?

GIVING AND RECEIVING FEEDBACK

Feedback is the communicative process of letting another person know that s/he has been understood. Feedback is an excellent source of learning because it helps us become more aware of what we do, how we do it, and the consequences that result from doing it. Moreover, feedback is a skill that can be developed and improved. Ultimately, feedback requires skill, risk, courage, understanding, empathy, and respect for yourself and others. The following are characteristics of the techniques of feedback.

1. <u>Feedback should relate to behavior not to the person.</u> Refer to what a person <u>does</u> rather than who that person <u>is</u>. In order to do this, use <u>adverbs</u> which relate to actions rather than <u>adjectives</u> (which relate to qualities). For example, don't say "he is obnoxious" when you can say "he talks a lot at parties." Making comments about a person doesn't lead to productive change, but focusing on behavior within a specific situation leads to the possibility of nonthreatening change.

2. <u>Make observations not inferences.</u> Observations are based on concrete facts and information. Inferences are conclusions or interpretations which follow our observations. Since inferences are often incorrect and bias our perceptions, keep these distinct from observations when providing feedback to another. When giving feedback, state your observations first ("I can't help but notice that your face is red, your hands are shaking, and your lips are pursed;"); then, if warranted, draw an inference ("You must be angry"). In other words, <u>describe</u> but don't <u>judge</u>.

3. <u>Feedback should relate to an immediate situation not an abstract or past situation.</u> Feedback is more meaningful, appropriate, and influential if it is concretely tied to a specific situation, present time, and present place. In addition, you should be sensitive to when feedback is given. Messages given at inappropriate times are ineffective and potentially harmful.

4. <u>Share information but don't give advise.</u> People should make their own decisions. Giving advise is an attempt to take away the other's choice. So, frame your feedback as information ("I don't like your boyfriend") rather than advice ("You should break up with that guy").

5. <u>Feedback should help identify alternatives not answers.</u> Since it is not your place to tell another what to do, your feedback is more likely to be productive if you provide interpretations that open up new possibilities or perceptions. Premature or quick solutions aren't very useful.

6. <u>Feedback should help the other, not you.</u> Sometimes we simply want to cathart or "get it off our chests." This information may give you a release, but it is not constructive to the other. Consequently, make sure that you take the needs of the other into consideration and offer, but do not impose, feedback.

7. <u>Don't overwhelm another with feedback.</u> We have a tendency to "unload" on the other once we begin to feed information to the other. If you overload the other with feedback, chances are that your information will not be effective. So, keep it short, simple, and appropriate.

14

INITIATING CONVERSATION

Goal: To identify specific communicative ways to open conversations.

Instructions: Initiating conversation is difficult because the initiator risks rejection. In addition, the initiator should begin conversation by balancing ritualized, predictable messages with creative ones. Form groups of 4-6 persons. Take each of the following scenarios and create opening lines to initiate interaction. Be prepared to justify your responses in a class discussion.

1. On your nightly jaunt in your neighborhood, you pass by a grandmother walking with her year-old granddaughter in a stroller.

2. You are in the produce department at the grocery store when you see a stranger you would like to meet and perhaps date.

3. You are in the waiting room at the local auto mechanic shop when a man you think was in your biology class last semester enters the room and sits down to wait for his car.

4. You attend the funeral of your boss. You have never met her husband or her parents yet you would like to offer your condolences.

5. You work at McDonalds and your Speech Communication instructor comes in and orders the Big Mac special.

6. You are being interviewed for your first job upon graduation from college. The interviewer takes you in to meet and talk with your prospective coworkers.

Discussion: How difficult was it to construct opening dialogues? Why? Was it difficult to balance expectations with creativity? If you had the choice, would you opt for a ritualized beginning or a creative beginning? Why? How important is nonverbal communication during the initiation of a conversation? Under what conditions should a handshake accompany your conversational opener?

It wasn't that difficult, the only thing that was difficult was to think of appropriate ones to share to the class. I would choose a ritualized beginning because I would think I know how the person would react. Nonverbal communication is very important because you don't want to say something but make your body or facial expressions say another. If it is formal you should make a handshake accompany a conversational opener.

COMPLIMENTING OTHERS

Goal: To develop and improve your ability to compliment another person.

Instructions: Your task is to say something nice about another person in class. You may compliment the person of your choice, and you may compliment her or him on anything that comes to your mind.

Discussion: Your discussion should center on a number of ideas. First, does your compliment differ depending upon how well you know the other person? In what specific ways? Are you uncomfortable with giving compliments? Is this a culturally-bound pattern? Are you equally as comfortable (or uncomfortable) receiving a compliment as you are giving a compliment? Why? When someone compliments you, are you likely to dismiss or accept the compliment? Do you wonder about the motivation or intentions of a person who compliments you? Why? Can you identify certain communicative skills that can aid you in the future in giving and receiving compliments?

IT'S HARD TO STOP TALKING

Goal: To experience the process of ending a conversation.

Instructions:

1. You will practice the following methods of ending a conversation:

   a. <u>Summary</u>--identifies the main points of the discussion: "I really understand how to organize this surprise party, Mom. I'll get started on the supplies right away."

   b. <u>Value</u>--a supportive statement that points out something that you found useful or are appreciative about: "This talk has helped so much! I really appreciate how much you've listened to my problem."

   c. <u>Future Interest</u>--identifies your desire to meet again: "I would really like to talk further with you about this. Could we get together later today?"

2. For each of the situations below, write an example of one of the three preceding methods of ending a conversation. Identify which type you are using.

   a. <u>Situation 1</u>: Disagreement with a parent. _____
   _____
   _____
   _____

   b. <u>Situation 2</u>: After listening to a close friend who talked about his troubled love life all evening. _____
   _____
   _____
   _____

   c. <u>Situation 3</u>: After an unenjoyable dinner date. _____
   _____
   _____
   _____

   d. <u>Situation 4</u>: After having a great date with someone you haven't seen in several years. _____
   _____
   _____
   _____

Discussion: Do you normally find it difficult to end conversations? Explain. Was it difficult to come up with these endings? Why or why not? How can using specific endings help your communication in your relationships?

Source: Linda A. Joesting, ed. <u>Communication: A Workbook for Interpersonal Communication</u>, 4th ed. Dubuque, Iowa: Kendall/Hunt, 1990, p. 328.

THE ARGUMENTATIVENESS SCALE

Goal: To identify the degree to which you tend to avoid or willingly approach situations in which controversial issues are argued.

Instructions: This questionnaire contains statements about arguing controversial issues. Argumentativeness "involves the tendency to advocate and refute positions on controversial issues." It is related to assertiveness rather than aggressiveness. Indicate how much each statement is true for you personally by placing the appropriate number in the blank to the left of the statement. Use the following key: 1 = almost never true; 2 = rarely true; 3 = occasionally true; 4 = often true; 5 = almost always true.

_____ 1. While in an argument, I worry that the person I am arguing with will form a negative impression of me.

_____ 2. Arguing over controversial issues improves my intelligence.

_____ 3. I enjoy avoiding arguments.

_____ 4. I am energetic and enthusiastic when I argue.

_____ 5. Once I finish an argument I promise myself that I will not get into another one.

_____ 6. Arguing with a person creates more problems for me than it solves.

_____ 7. I have a pleasant, good feeling when I win a point in an argument.

_____ 8. When I finish arguing with someone I feel nervous and upset.

_____ 9. I enjoy a good argument over a controversial issue.

_____ 10. I get an unpleasant feeling when I realize I am about to get into an argument.

_____ 11. I enjoy defending my point of view on an issue.

_____ 12. I am happy when I keep an argument from happening.

_____ 13. I do not like to miss the opportunity to argue a controversial issue.

_____ 14. I prefer being with people who rarely disagree with me.

_____ 15. I consider an argument an exciting intellectual challenge.

_____ 16. I find myself unable to think of effective points during an argument.

_____ 17. I feel refreshed and satisfied after an argument on a controversial issue.

_____ 18. I have the ability to do well in an argument.

_____ 19. I try to avoid getting into arguments.

_____ 20. I feel excitement when I expect that a conversation I am in is leading to an argument.

Scoring Instructions:

1. Add scores on items 2, 4, 7, 9, 11, 13, 15, 17, 18, and 20 to identify your tendency to _approach_ argumentative situations.

2. Add scores on items 1, 3, 5, 6, 8, 10, 12, 14, 16, and 19 to identify your tendency to _avoid_ argumentative situations.

3. Subtract the total of the 10 tendency to avoid items from the total of the 10 tendency to approach items to discover your _argumentativeness trait_.

4. Scores from   0 to -13 = low avoiding;   0 to 13 = low approaching
   -14 to -27 = moderate avoiding; 14 to 27 = moderate approaching
   -28 to -40 = high avoiding;   28 to 40 = high approaching

Source: Dominic A. Infante, and Andrew S. Rancer. "A conceptualization and Measure of Argumentativeness." _Journal of Personality Assessment_, 46 (1982): 76.

VERBAL AGGRESSIVENESS SCALE

Goal: To identify the degree to which your verbal communication is aggressive in nature or function.

Instructions: Verbal aggression consists of "attacking the self-concept of another person." They are "put-downs," character attacks, competence attacks, insults, ridicule, and profanity, all of which are designed to hurt, anger, irritate, embarrass, or discourage another. Chronic use of verbally aggressive messages can lead to relationship deterioration or termination. The following survey is concerned with how we try to get people to comply with our wishes. Indicate how often each statement is true for you personally when you try to influence other persons.

Use the following scale for items 1 - 10: 1 = almost never true; 2 = rarely true; 3 = occasionally true; 4 = often true; 5 = almost always true.

_____ 1.   When individuals are very stubborn, I use insults to soften the stubbornness.

_____ 2.   When people refuse to do a task I know is important, without good reason, I tell them they are unreasonable.

_____ 3.   If individuals I am trying to influence really deserve it, I attack their character.

_____ 4.   When people behave in ways that are in very poor taste, I insult them in order to shock them into proper behavior.

_____ 5.   When people simply will not budge on a matter of importance, I lose my temper and say rather strong things to them.

_____ 6.   When individuals insult me, I get a lot of pleasure out of really telling them off.

_____ 7.   I like poking fun at people who do things which are very stupid in order to stimulate their intelligence.

_____ 8.   When people do things which are mean or cruel, I attack their character in order to help correct their behavior.

_____ 9.   When nothing seems to work in trying to influence others, I yell and scream in order to get some movement from them.

_____ 10. When I am not able to refute others' positions, I try to make them feel defensive in order to weaken their positions.

Use the following scale for items 11 - 20: 5 = almost never true; 4 = rarely true; 3 = occasionally true; 2 = often true; 1 = almost always true.

_____ 11. I am extremely careful to avoid attacking individuals' intelligence when I attack their ideas.

_____ 12. I try very hard to avoid having other people feel bad about themselves when I try to influence them.

_____ 13. When others do things I regard as stupid, I try to be extremely gentle with them.

_____ 14. I try to make people feel good about themselves even when their ideas are stupid.

_____ 15. When people criticize my shortcomings, I take it in good humor and do not try to get back at them.

_____ 16. When I dislike individuals greatly, I try not to show it in what I say or how I say it.

_____ 17. When I attack persons' ideas, I try not to damage their self-concepts.

_____ 18. When I try to influence people, I make a great effort not to offend them.

_____ 19. I refuse to participate in arguments when they involve personal attacks.

_____ 20. When an argument shifts to personal attacks, I try very hard to change the subject.

Scoring Instructions: Add your scores together for all 20 items.

A score from 20 - 46 = low verbal aggressiveness
A score from 47 - 74 = moderate verbal aggressiveness
A score from 75 - 100 = high verbal aggressiveness

Discussion: Since verbal aggressiveness is an attack upon another's self-concept or worth, the higher your score, the more likely you are to hurt, anger, embarrass, or discourage another. As a class, figure out what conditions prompt a person to verbally "put-down" another, and what usually happens as a result of the aggressive message. To what degree do these kinds of messages damage relationships? Try to identify concrete communicative ways of repairing the damage of a verbal attack; also identify communicative ways to respond to another's verbal attack.

Source: Dominic A. Infante, and Charles J. Wigley III. "Verbal Aggressiveness: An Interpersonal Model and Measure." Communication Monographs, 53 (1986): 61 - 69.

OBSERVING NONVERBAL BEHAVIORS

Goal: This exercise is designed to identify the pervasiveness of types of nonverbal behaviors in routine conversations.

Instructions:

1. Pair up with another classmate and observe persons interacting with one another on campus or another public setting.

2. Find one example of six of the following eight types of nonverbal behaviors:

    a. <u>emblem</u> (gesture that has a direct verbal equivalent--i.e., "OK" sign, "time out" sign)
    b. <u>illustrator</u> (behavior that describes properties of something you are explaining verbally--i.e., directions)
    c. <u>affect display</u> (facial expression showing emotion)
    d. <u>regulator</u> (behavior that controls the flow of conversation--i.e., eye contact, head nod, hand gesture accompanying verbal)
    e. <u>body type</u> (ectomorph, mesomorph, endomorph)
    f. <u>paralanguage/vocalics</u> (use of the voice to convey meaning)
    g. <u>proxemics</u> (use of space to define territory or relationship)
    h. <u>artifacts</u> (use of material possessions to convey status or meaning)

3. Write a description of each encounter. Do so by identifying the specific nonverbal behaviors observed, and draw inferences about the nature of their relationship, the substance of their conversation, and the emotions of the interactants.

    <u>Example</u>: Artifacts

    <u>Description</u>: Two female students are sitting together at the student union. One is applying lipstick while the other stares at her rings. Both are wearing designer jeans and Nikes. They are laughing, and are seated in a relaxed posture.

    <u>Inference</u>: The women are likely concerned about their appearance, and seem to be friends. Chances are they are talking about men.

Discussion: Discussion issues should surround whether you and your classmates discovered similar, recurrent forms or types of nonverbal behavior. In addition, to what degree would you say that your assessment of the meaning of each nonverbal behavior is accurate?

THE INFLUENCE OF THE ENVIRONMENT

Goal: The purpose of this exercise is to help you understand how the physical environment affects your communication.

Instructions:

1.   Complete this assignment with either a partner involved in a long-term relationship or another acquaintance.

2.   Meet with your partner in two contrasting settings. For example, you may meet in the lobby of a dorm, a fast food restaurant, your parent's living room, or a health spa. Your task while in each setting is to prepare a Christmas party, including a list of the guests who will attend, the complete menu for dinner, and any additional activities for the evening (i.e., carols, tree decorating).

Discussion: After both experiences, evaluate how your attitude, approach, and outcome of the task and your communication behavior varied as a result of the environment. For example, how much time was devoted to the task as opposed to other social conversation? Was the task more enjoyable in one setting versus another? Did your seating arrangements differ in each setting? Did you notice any other dynamics affecting your interaction?

SEATING ARRANGEMENTS

Goal: The purpose of this exercise is to identify comfortable proxemic seating distances among persons as well as how we respond to those who violate our space.

Instructions: Chairs will be set up in front of the class. You will be called upon to arrange them in relation to each other according to the situations listed below. As the class obverves, adjust the arrangement of the chairs to fit the following cases.

1. There are four chairs available. Two people who don't know each other come into the waiting room of a dentist.

2. Two good friends are seated at a restaurant.

3. A mother and her sick 10-year-old child wait at the pediatrician's office.

4. A boss calls in a secretary to complain about his sloppy letter writing.

5. A supervisor calls in a subordinate to compliment her on her excellent work. Arrange them around the supervisor's desk.

6. You enter your boss' office to request a transfer to another department.

7. Devise your own situation and arrange the chairs according to how close or far away participants are likely to sit.

Discussion: Class members should be consulted on the placement of persons in relation to one another and any differences they would make to your configuration. Discussion should center around whether status and the relative privacy of the setting affect space arrangements. In addition, is personal space culturally bound? Where did you learn how far away to sit from someone else? What information is being conveyed by such seating arrangements--i.e., what are you telling others and what do their choices tell you?

SHAKING HANDS

Goal: To identify the meaning and consequences of shaking hands.

Instructions: You will introduce yourself to another class member, using a handshake during your introduction. Repeat this introduction five times with the following five handshakes.

1.   a firm confident handshake

2.   a limp, "dead-fish" handshake

3.   an active, pump-handle shake

4.   a delicate fingertip handshake

5.   a "bruiser" or bone-crusher handshake

Discussion: Discussion should center on whether you had trouble performing any of the kinds of handshakes and whether you have encountered them in your experience. In addition, are any gender differences relevant for any of these handshakes? What verbal and nonverbal behaviors are likely to accompany each kind of handshake? Is your attitude toward other persons affected by the way they shake hands?

PERSONAL SPACE

Goal: The purposes of this exercise are to determine what personal space is, what your personal space is, and what your feelings are about personal space when it is invaded.

Instructions:

1. Form groups of 2 males and 2 females. With your partners, perform each of the following at least twice. As you do this, examine your "feelings" or emotional responses.

2. Have a person of the same sex approach you from each of the following directions. Stop him or her when the distance between you is comfortable. Measure and record the approximate distance.

   a. Directly from the front
   b. Directly from the right
   c. Directly from the left
   d. Directly from the rear

3. Repeat the same exercises with a person of the opposite sex.

4. Repeat the same exercises as above, except this time allow the person to come too close. At one of the positions, engage the person in conversation for at least one full minute.

Discussion: Discussion should surround what differences direction makes in feelings of comfort, what differences gender makes in perceptions of space violations, and in what ways you altered your behavior to compensate for violations of your space.

TOUCH AND
INTERPERSONAL INTERACTIONS

Goal: To compare your touching behavior with that of research on interpersonal touch.

Instructions: The following is a personal assessment of where you get touched. The person who touches you and the region of touch on your body are listed on the chart. The region numbers appear on the figure at the right. Identify who touched you where. Compare your results with the research findings summarized below.

Region	Close Same-Sex Friend	Close Opposite-Sex Friend	Your Mother	Your Father
1				
2				
3				
4				
5				
6				
7				
8				
9				

1. **Males Reported These Results in the Research**:

    a. Close-same-sex friend: regions 2, 3, 8, 9, had the most touch
    b. Close-opposite-sex friend: all regions had a great deal of touch
    c. Mother: regions 1, 2, 3, 4, and 8 had a great deal of touch
    d. Father: regions 2, 3, and 4 had the most touch

2. **Females Reported These Results in the Research**:

    a. Close-same-sex friend: regions 1, 2, 3, 4, 5, and 9 had the most touch
    b. Close-opposite-sex friend: all regions had a great deal of touch
    c. Mother: regions 1, 2, 3, 4, 5, 6, and 7 had a great deal of touch
    d. Father: 1, 2, 3, and 4 had the most touch

Discussion: What role does touch play in developing, maintaining, and strengthening relationships? Are we socialized to touch or not touch? In what ways? Can you distinguish touches which relate to intimacy versus affection needs?

Source: L. B. Rosenfield, S. Kartus, and C. Ray. "Body Accessibility Revisited." Journal of Communication, 26 (1976): 27-30.

26

THE INFLUENCE OF BODY TYPE

Goal: To identify the degree to which your body type influences your communication.

Instructions: Answer each of the statements below by circling the one word out of the three that you believe most closely describes you. When you are done, add up the total number of circles in each column.

	A	B	C
1.	dependent	interdependent	independent
2.	relaxed	confident	anxious
3.	extroverted	social	introverted
4.	sluggish	competent	precise
5.	cooperative	assertive	cautious
6.	agreeable	efficient	sensitive
7.	close	social	detached
8.	submissive	dominant	suspicious
9.	light-hearted	optimistic	serious
10.	sympathetic	considerate	callous

Total _____   _____   _____

Discussion: According to William Sheldon, three basic dimensions of the human physique together constitute a person's somatotype (body type): endomorph, mesomorph, and ectomorph. Each body type tends to correlate with a particular temperament.

A. The Endomorph: Soft, round, fat. The endomorph was rated fatter, older, shorter, more old-fashioned, less strong physically, less good-looking, more talkative, more warm-hearted and sympathetic, more good-natured and agreeable, more dependent on others, and trusting of others.

B. The Mesomorph: Bony, muscular, athletic. The mesomorph was rated stronger, more masculine, better looking, more adventurous, younger, taller, more mature in behavior, and more self-reliant.

C. The Ectomorph: Tall, thin, fragile. The ectomorph was rated thinner, younger, more ambitious, taller, more suspicious of others, more tense and nervous, less masculine, more stubborn and inclined to be difficult, more pessimistic, and quieter.

What is the relationship between actual body shape and scores on the test? How accurately do you feel your temperament scores respond to your body type? What happens to the personality of an individual who is stereotyped as an endomorph? As an ectomorph? How does the stereotyping of body shape and temperament affect the way in which a person communicates with others?

INFLUENCES ON COMMUNICATION

Perception

Interpersonal Needs

Self-Image

Interpersonal Attraction

Emotions and Apprehension

PERCEIVING YOUR SELF

Goal: The purpose of this exercise is to describe your own image of your strengths and weaknesses.

Instructions: Think about how you interact with your family, friends, intimates, and coworkers. Then, complete each of the following sentences with a description of your perception of yourself.

1. I am glad that I am _____.

2. I am glad that I am _____.

3. I am glad that I am not _____.

4. I am glad that I am not _____.

5. I wish I was not _____.

6. I wish I was not _____.

7. I wish I could be _____.

8. I wish I could be _____.

Discussion: Did you have an easier time identifying your weaknesses rather than your strengths? Are they more obvious? Would others describe you in the same way? In other words, to what degree would you say you frequently communicate these characteristics to others? Can you come up with suggestions for reinforcing those characteristics which are strengths and diminishing those characteristics which you perceived as weaknesses?

HOW SENSITIVE ARE YOU?

Goal: To help you realize that sensitivity determines how a person will perceive and communicate.

Instructions: Complete the Sensitivity Self-Report Scale below. When you are done, add up your scores for each of the three sections. The area in which you earn the lowest score is the area in which you are the most sensitive. Then, form groups of 4-6 persons. Discuss your responses and try to come up with a definition of sensitivity.

Rating Scale:
- 1 = very highly sensitive to; very important, could change your actions
- 2 = sensitive to; matters and may modify, but won't impede actions
- 3 = aware of; will take into consideration but will not let it affect actions at all
- 4 = not very aware of; don't really pay much attention to, it's of little importance
- 5 = not aware of; does not really matter

SELF:

How sensitive are you towards	Circle response
1. your appearance	1 2 3 4 5
2. your mental attitude	1 2 3 4 5
3. tension	1 2 3 4 5
4. your physical health	1 2 3 4 5
5. bodily symptoms	1 2 3 4 5
6. your creativity and assets	1 2 3 4 5
7. your awareness	1 2 3 4 5
8. alertness	1 2 3 4 5
9. motivation	1 2 3 4 5
10. fatigue	1 2 3 4 5
11. your failures	1 2 3 4 5
12. your successes	1 2 3 4 5
13. your fears	1 2 3 4 5
14. your personal problems	1 2 3 4 5
15. decisions you must make	1 2 3 4 5
16. your opinions of others	1 2 3 4 5
17. your behavior toward others	1 2 3 4 5
18. your verbal communication	1 2 3 4 5
19. your body language	1 2 3 4 5
20. your shortcomings	1 2 3 4 5
21. your personality	1 2 3 4 5
22. your handicaps	1 2 3 4 5
23. your position and status	1 2 3 4 5
24. intrapersonal competition	1 2 3 4 5
25. your aptitude	1 2 3 4 5

OTHER PEOPLE:

How sensitive are you toward   **Circle response**

1.	your family's problems	1	2	3	4	5
2.	your spouse's feelings and needs	1	2	3	4	5
3.	your job requirements	1	2	3	4	5
4.	colleagues' opinions of you	1	2	3	4	5
5.	criticism of you	1	2	3	4	5
6.	criticism of things you do	1	2	3	4	5
7.	society's ills	1	2	3	4	5
8.	mass movements	1	2	3	4	5
9.	fads	1	2	3	4	5
10.	smoking	1	2	3	4	5
11.	drinking	1	2	3	4	5
12.	obnoxious behavior	1	2	3	4	5
13.	changes in plans	1	2	3	4	5
14.	appearances	1	2	3	4	5
15.	personalities	1	2	3	4	5
16.	others' strong points	1	2	3	4	5
17.	others' shortcomings	1	2	3	4	5
18.	others' handicaps	1	2	3	4	5
19.	educational level	1	2	3	4	5
20.	position and status	1	2	3	4	5
21.	achievements	1	2	3	4	5
22.	competing with you	1	2	3	4	5
23.	judgments of you	1	2	3	4	5
24.	compliments of you	1	2	3	4	5
25.	advice to you	1	2	3	4	5

OTHER VARIABLES:

How sensitive are you toward   **Circle response**

1.	parties	1	2	3	4	5
2.	politics	1	2	3	4	5
3.	environment	1	2	3	4	5
4.	money issues	1	2	3	4	5
5.	weather	1	2	3	4	5
6.	sunshine	1	2	3	4	5
7.	crowded places	1	2	3	4	5
8.	arguments	1	2	3	4	5
9.	meetings	1	2	3	4	5
10.	school counselors	1	2	3	4	5
11.	colors	1	2	3	4	5
12.	smells	1	2	3	4	5
13.	visual stimulation	1	2	3	4	5
14.	smog	1	2	3	4	5
15.	disappointment	1	2	3	4	5
16.	changes of plans	1	2	3	4	5
17.	the media	1	2	3	4	5
18.	poverty	1	2	3	4	5
19.	art forms	1	2	3	4	5
20.	religion	1	2	3	4	5

OTHER VARIABLES (cont.)

How sensitive are you toward   Circle response

21. music | 1 | 2 | 3 | 4 | 5
22. death | 1 | 2 | 3 | 4 | 5
23. sex | 1 | 2 | 3 | 4 | 5
24. television | 1 | 2 | 3 | 4 | 5
25. newspapers | 1 | 2 | 3 | 4 | 5

OVERALL ASSESSMENT:

_____ 1.   I am very aware of myself.
_____ 2.   I am sensitive to others.
_____ 3.   I need positive reinforcement from others.
_____ 4.   Others' opinions of me really make a difference.
_____ 5.   I don't care what others think of me, but I am sensitive to their needs and how I might help them.
_____ 6.   I am basically an individualist.

Discussion: Are you basically a sensitive person? Are you more sensitive to yourself or to others? What part does perception play in sensitivity? Do you see any way in which your sensitivity hampers you? How does your sensitivity help you? How do you feel about your overall sensitiveness? Is there any area in which you would like to increase your sensitivity? How might that be accomplished?

Source: Linda A. Joesting, ed. Communication: A Workbook for Interpersonal Communication, 4th ed. Dubuque, Iowa: Kendall/Hunt, 1990, pp. 183-186.

ANIMAL PERCEPTION EXERCISE

Goal: The purpose of this exercise is to demonstrate that our perceptions of ourselves are different than others' perceptions of us. In addition, this exercise identifies multiple levels of perceptions and meta-perceptions ("meta" means something upon itself; here it means a perception about a perception).

Instructions: Pair off with a classmate. Your instructor will provide you with a topic that the two of you should discuss for approximately ten minutes. At the end of this interaction, complete the following information. After you are done, compare your answers to your partners' answers and discuss similarities and differences in your respective responses.

1. **Self-Image**: Assign yourself an animal that you think best expresses or symbolizes who you think you are.

2. **Other-Image**: Assign your partner an animal that you think best expresses or symbolizes who you think your partner is.

3. **Meta-Self-Image**: Assign an animal to yourself that you believe your partner assigned to you. In other words, what animal do you think your partner assigned to you?

4. **Meta-Other-Image**: Assign your partner an animal that you think your partner assigned to her/himself. In other words, what animal do you think your partner assigned to him/herself?

Discussion: Discussion about this exercise should center on why different animals were assigned at each level of perception; what clues (verbal, nonverbal) led you to the assigning of various animals; what communication problems might result from each other's different perceptions; and how such perceptual problems might be diminished or overcome.

INTERPERSONAL PERCEPTION METHOD

Goal: The Interpersonal Perception Method is a technique for analyzing perceptions in a dyadic relationship. The assumption underlying the method is that the behavior of each person toward the other is mediated by the perceptions and experiences each has of the other.

A.   **Three Perspectives:**

   1.   **Direct Perspective:**   "I see myself."

   2.   **Meta-Perspective:**   "I see you."

   3.   **Meta-Meta-Perspective:**   "I see you seeing me."

Example

	WIFE	HUSBAND
DIRECT	"I don't like cooking.	I don't like cooking.
META	He doesn't like cooking.	She doesn't like cooking.
META-META	He knows I don't like cooking.	She knows I don't like cooking.

B.   **Four Ways to Assess a Relationship**

   1.   Comparison of <u>Direct Perspectives</u> yields <u>Agreement or Disagreement</u>: For example, "I don't like cooking" and "I don't like cooking" yields agreement about each's attitude toward cooking.

   2.   Comparison of <u>Meta-Perspective</u> and <u>Direct Perspective</u> yields <u>Understanding or Misunderstanding</u>:   For example, the wife's "He doesn't like cooking," and the husband's "I don't like cooking" yields understanding about the husband's perception of cooking.

   3.   Comparison of one's own <u>Direct-Perspective</u> and <u>Meta-Meta Perspective</u> yields <u>Feelings of Being Understood or Misunderstood</u>: For example, the wife's "I don't like cooking" and her "He knows I don't like cooking" yields feelings of being understood.

   4.   Comparison of <u>Meta-Meta Perspective</u> and <u>Meta-Perspective</u> yields <u>Realization or Failure of Realization</u>:   For example, the wife's "He knows I don't like cooking" and the husband's "She doesn't like cooking" means that she realizes that he understands her attitude.

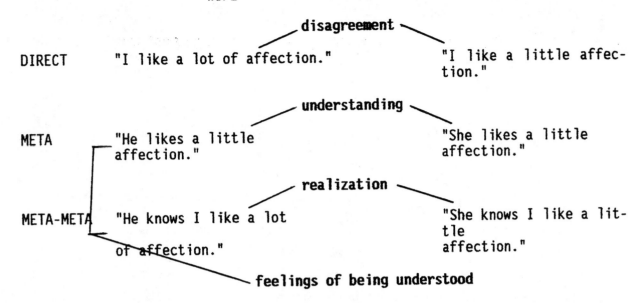

C. Implications and Uses of the Interpersonal Perception Method

1. It tells you what you know and don't know and what perceptions you're acting upon, perhaps inaccurately. If you say "I think" to any part of the model or if you must leave a portion blank, then either you don't know or you're operating on limited, inaccurate information.

2. It tells you which of your perceptions need to be checked out for accuracy.

3. Over time, it may tell you your patterns of interpersonal perception. That is, what parts of the model do you usually not know about another person, or what do others usually not know about you?

4. The method can accommodate both the content and relational dimensions of communication. The content dimension can be plotted out for any subject. If doing so does not produce understanding of a problem, look to the relational level (relational issues surround power, affection, inclusion, attention, competence, self-worth, etc.) If you know the issue, plot it out; if you don't, plot all relational issues out until the real issue surfaces.

5. It also explains why your behavior is the way it is. If you think someone feels a certain way, you will subsequently respond to that person based on your perceptions.

6. To create accuracy, asking the other is the easiest way. If asking is risky, look to other behavioral clues in order to check the validity of your perceptions.

Source: R. D. Laing, H. Phillipson, and A. R. Lee. Interpersonal Perception: A Theory and a Method of Research. New York: Springer, 1966: p. 62.

TESTING YOUR PERCEPTIONS

Goal: The purpose of this activity is to identify perceptual biases and to generate skills in testing your perceptions.

Instructions: Our perceptions are subjective, biased, incomplete, and often self-fulfilling. As a result, we have the tendency to draw erroneous inferences about others' behavior. You can create more accurate perceptions, however, by learning the following three skills. Testing your perceptions requires that you do three things.

1.   Describe behaviors you observe in others. In other words, tell the other person what you have seen her/him say or do. This clarifies the behaviors you are perceiving.

2.   Interpret behaviors by creating two different meanings or reasons that account for them. If you can attribute two possible interpretations of another's behavior, this will stop you from assuming that your first interpretation is the only correct one.

3.   Request feedback from the other person about the accuracy of your interpretations. Allow the other person to verify this accuracy by agreeing, disagreeing, or providing another alternate perception. In other words, ask the other person whether your impressions are valid.

Example: "When you didn't show up at 7:00 p.m. like you said you would (behavior), I wasn't sure whether you had forgotton (first interpretation) or decided it wasn't important (second interpretation). Why didn't you keep our appointment (request for feedback)."

Exercise: Test your own perceptions by applying the three skills above to the situations given you below. Keep in mind that the purpose of this activity is to discover the accuracy of your perceptions. So, you may well find out that your initial impressions were wrong.

1.   You were not invited to attend one of your closest friend's graduation party.

2.   Your neighbor's son continues to park his car in a spot that blocks most of your driveway even though you have requested repeatedly that this stop.

3.   You are working on a group project for a class. One student has been given the responsibility to research your group's topic and report back to the group in a week. Two weeks have gone by and this student still has not contacted the group about this research.

4.   Devise an example from your own experience. Describe the situation and the perceptual distortions that might have resulted. Then test your perceptions to see if a different interpretation emerges.

Discussion: Discussion should surround the degree to which our perceptions are normally accurate or inaccurate; what accounts for the perceptions we form? How much of your own ego or needs determines the perceptions you create? What likely consequences will perception checking have on your interpersonal relationships?

3.   Each of the three needs--openness or affection, control, and inclusion has two subparts: one is <u>how you behave</u> (i.e., "I include people"), the other is <u>how others behave toward you</u> (i.e., "People include me"). In general, you should behave toward others the way you would like them to behave toward you in order to meet your needs.

4.   This questionnaire is not an evaluation. There is nothing good or bad about any score. Scores are opportunities to learn more about yourself. Your scores are a reflection of how you have chosen to be, up to now. You can change if you have the desire and the willingness to learn how to change. The primary value of this instrument is as a springboard. You learn from observing your responses to the scores. These responses may tell you more about yourself. When you find yourself responding angrily or defensively to one of the scores, consider the possibility that, deep down, you believe the score is accurate and you do not want it to be. Or consider that only one percent is accurate. Is there something you can learn from that one percent? If the scores do not fit the picture you have of yourself, you may assume (a) the questionnaire is inaccurate, or (b) the part of you that responded to the items is telling you something about yourself you have not been paying attention to, or (c) there is some truth in both "a" and "b" above. In short, if you avoid seeing these scores as judgments, you may experience the joy that comes from getting to know yourself a little better.

Source: Will Schutz. <u>Element B Behavior: A FIRO Instrument</u>. Mill Valley, CA: Will Schutz Associates, 1992.

INTERPERSONAL COMMUNICATION FEUD

<u>Goal</u>: To introduce you to the interpersonal needs of affection, inclusion, and control.

<u>Definitions</u>: <u>Affection</u> is a need to give and receive love, liking, and attention. <u>Inclusion</u> is a need to belong, be a member of a group, and include others in your social life. <u>Control</u> is a need to dominate, to direct others, to stand out, and to let others make decisions.

<u>Instructions</u>:

1. Take out a piece of paper and draw <u>three</u> horizontal lines. These lines are each a continuum with a low end of zero and a high end of ten. On the first line, rank yourself on your need for <u>affection</u> (10 would be the highest need for affection, 0 would be the lowest possible need). On the second line, rank yourself from 0 - 10 on your need for <u>inclusion</u>; on the third line, rank youself from 0 - 10 on your need for <u>control</u>. Be honest, but try to avoid taking the middle position of 5.

2. <u>Three</u> students will be asked to come to the front of the class with their continua, a pencil, and a large name tag to set down in full view of the class. Your instructor will ask you to write down answers to <u>two</u> additional questions. These questions are designed to elicit moderate self-disclosure and will range from more serious questions (i.e., "The most important thing I expect to learn from this class is _____") to less serious questions (i.e., "The main reason I came to this university is _____"). Your instructor will collect the answers from all three students and then read the answers without revealing the author. The class is asked to predict which answers belong with which students. Class members who guess correctly receive <u>one</u> point. At this point, three new students will come to the front of the class and the game will proceed until all students have participated. The student or students with the highest point totals will be acknowledged and will receive an award to be determined by your instructor.

<u>Discussion</u>: Discussion should center on the nature of interpersonal needs, and how they influence our behavior. In addition, you should discover how others perceive your interpersonal needs. To what degree did your own perception of your interpersonal needs match the perceptions of other class members?

<u>Source</u>: David Williams. "Interpersonal Communication Feud." <u>Speech Communication Teacher</u>, 4 (1990): 8-9.

SELF-ESTEEM

Goal: This exercise tries to identify your level of self-esteem. Self-esteem is the degree to which you feel positive toward or accepting of yourself.

Instructions: Rate yourself on the following scales by placing an "I" in the spot that best reflects your _ideal_ image of where you would like to be. Then, place an "R" in the spot for each item that best reflects where you _really_ think you are at the present time. Your self-esteem is the difference between the two sets of scores on each item. The larger the discrepancies, the lower the self-esteem; the smaller the discrepancies, the higher the self-esteem.

Secure about Values	— — — — —	Insecure about Values
Accepts Self	— — — — —	Cannot Accept Self
Happy	— — — — —	Unhappy
Contented	— — — — —	Discontented
Tries Successfully	— — — — —	Fails at Endeavors
Includes Others	— — — — —	Dependent on Others
Takes Risks	— — — — —	Afraid of Risks
Makes Friends	— — — — —	Is Isolated
Trusts Others	— — — — —	Is Distrustful
Is Cooperative	— — — — —	Is Possessive of
with Others		Others
Follows Rules	— — — — —	Makes Demands
Is Responsible	— — — — —	Withdraws or
for Behavior		Aggresses
Talks Freely	— — — — —	Seldom Talks
Independent	— — — — —	Often Frustrated

Discussion: Generally, a person with low self-esteem is cynical, pessimistic, and talks negatively about the self, has difficulty accepting praise or compliments, is defensive, blaming, and anxious, and tends to whine. Persons with high self-esteem are able to compliment others' accomplishment, do not need constant reinforcement about their worth, take risks, don't spend inordinate amounts of time talking about themselves, are confident but not condescending, take credit and/or blame when warranted, and are optimistic, flexible, and accepting of others. To what degree do you fit either of these characterizations? Can you identify any communication patterns that result from your feelings about yourself? If you could make one change in your self-esteem, what would that be and what communication behaviors could you adopt to make that change happen?

DISCLOSING YOUR SELF-CONCEPT

Goal: To identify and disclose important components of your image of yourself, and to look at the interdependence of one's self-concept and one's communicative roles.

Instructions: Your task is to compose a visual image of your self-concept by constructing a poster board. Peruse magazines, newspapers, mailings, flyers, and other written materials. From these sources, cut out letters, symbols, and pictures that represent self-concept elements contained in the qusetions below. There are no limitations on size, color, or shape of the poster board, so be creative and have fun. Be prepared to present this form of your self-concept to the class.

1. What is your first and last name?
2. What are some descriptive words or images that depict the social role with which you identify?
3. What are your goals and dreams?
4. What are your strengths?
5. What are your weaknesses?
6. Choose an animal that you can most identify with.
7. What was your most embarrassing moment?
8. Delineate the best day of your life.
9. Identify the worst day of your life.
10. What are some of your hobbies?
11. When were you born and what else happened on that day?
12. What is the subject of your recurring daydreams?
13. Who is in your family and what is your family like?
14. What is your religious affiliation and how important is it in your life?
15. What central moral principle guides your life?

Discussion: After sharing your poster boards, the class discussion should surround what elements comprise one's self-concept. Are certain dimensions more important than others? What are they? Is it really possible to communicate one's whole self to others? Is there a difference between your image of yourself and others' image of you? What are these differences, if any? Can communication alter one's self-concept? If so, how?

Source: Ms. Jennifer Graber, Department of Speech Communication, California State University, Long Beach.

INTERPERSONAL ATTRACTION
INVENTORY

Instructions: Interpersonal attraction consists of three interrelated elements--task attraction, physical attraction, and social attraction. According to McCroskey and McCain (p. 261), "the more people are attracted to one another, the more they will communicate with one another; and the more we are attracted to another person, the more influence that person has on us in interpersonal communication." Either think of a person you know or interact with a class member about any subject for twenty minutes. Then answer the statements below using the following key:

Scoring Key:
  Mark 5 if you strongly agree
  Mark 4 if you agree
  Mark 3 if you neither agree nor disagree
  Mark 2 if you disagree
  Mark 1 if you strongly disagree

Social Attraction

_____ 1. I think s/he could be a friend of mine.
_____ 2. It would be easy to meet and talk with him/her.
_____ 3. S/he sould fit into my circle of friends.
_____ 4. We could establish a personal friendship with each other.
_____ 5. I would like to have a friendly chat with him/her.

Physical Attraction

_____ 6. I think s/he is quite pretty/handsome.
_____ 7. S/he is very sexy looking.
_____ 8. I find him/her very attractive physically.
_____ 9. I like the way s/he looks.
_____ 10. I don't find him/her somewhat ugly.

Task Attraction

_____ 11. S/he is not a typical goof-off when assigned a job to do.
_____ 12. I have confidence in his/her ability to get the job done.
_____ 13. If I wanted to get things done, I could probably depend on him/her.
_____ 14. I could get anything accomplished with him/her.
_____ 15. S/he would be a good problem solver.

Results:
  56 - 75 = high attractiveness
  36 - 55 = moderate attractiveness
  15 - 35 = low attractiveness

Discussion: What is your definition of interpersonal attraction? Is one dimension more important than another in assessing attraction? How does your level of attraction toward another affect your communication with her/him?

Source: James C. McCroskey and Thomas A. McCain. "The Measurement of Interpersonal Attraction." _Speech Monographs_, 41 (1974): 261-266.

INTERPERSONAL ATTRACTION IDEALS

Goal: To identify your ideal conception of attraction, and to identify attractive qualities in the opposite sex.

Instructions: Complete each of the statements below individually. Then form groups of 4 - 6 persons and try to arrive at a consensus with your responses.

1. Identify five characteristics that make a member of the opposite sex attractive. _____
_____
_____

2. Identify five characteristics that make a member of the opposite sex repulsive. _____
_____
_____

3. Identify five characteristics that make a member of your own sex attractive. _____
_____
_____

4. Identify five characteristics that make a member of your own sex repulsive. _____
_____
_____

5. Think of the person with whom you are presently intimately involved (or think about your most recent past intimate relationship). Name five qualities that attracted you to this person. _____
_____
_____

6. Think of the person with whom you are presently intimately involved (or think about your most recent past intimate relationship). Name five qualities that repulsed you about this person. _____
_____
_____

Discussion: Can you come up with an encompassing definition for interpersonal attraction? Was it easier to list repulsive characteristics than attractive qualities? Are there any gender differences in what constitutes attraction toward another? Is your criteria for attraction different if you are describing a friend as opposed to an intimate? Did your concept of what is attractive change during the development of the relationship? In other words, are you attracted to your intimate other for different reasons now than at the beginning of your relationship?

EMOTIONS

Goal: To identify which emotions you can express and have difficulty expressing, and to look at the effects of communicating or withholding emotions.

Instructions: Identify the degree to which you feel comfortable expressing the following emotions by placing your response in the space next to the emotion named. Then, complete the statements accompanying each emotion. Use this scale to determine your response:

    5 = expressing this emotion is very easy
    4 = expressing this emotion is sometimes easy
    3 = expressing this emotion is just as easy as it is difficult
    2 = expressing this emotion is sometimes difficult
    1 = expressing this emotion is very difficult

____ 1. **LOVE:** Showing love is like _____

_____

____ 2. **DISGUST:** I get disgusted when _____

_____

____ 3. **SADNESS:** I am most sad when _____

_____

____ 4. **DISAPPOINTMENT:** I get disappointed when _____

_____

____ 5. **ANGER:** I get so angry when _____

_____

____ 6. **EXCITEMENT:** Nothing makes me more excited than ___

_____

____ 7. **FEAR:** I am most afraid when _____

_____

____ 8. **JOY:** I have never felt so much joy than when _____

_____

____ 9. **PRIDE:** I felt more pride when _____

_____

____ 10. **CARE:** When I care I _____

_____

Discussion: Is it harder for you to express "negative" emotions than "positive" emotions? What emotion can you express easiest? What emotion is most difficult for you to express? Why?

PERSONAL REPORT OF COMMUNICATION
APPREHENSION (PRCA-24)

Directions: This instrument is composed of twenty-four statements concerning feelings about communicating with other people. Please indicate the degree to which each statement applies to you by marking whether you (1) strongly agree, (2) agree, (3) are undecided, (4) disagree, or (5) strongly disagree. Please just record your first impression.

_____ 1.   I dislike participating in group discussions.

_____ 2.   Generally, I am comfortable while participating in a group discussion.

_____ 3.   I am tense and nervous while participating in group discussions.

_____ 4.   I like to get involved in group discussions.

_____ 5.   Engaging in a group discussion with new people makes me tense and nervous.

_____ 6.   I am calm and relaxed while participating in group discussions.

_____ 7.   Generally, I am nervous when I have to participate in a meeting.

_____ 8.   Usually I am calm and relaxed while participating in meetings.

_____ 9.   I am very calm and relaxed when I am called upon to express an opinion at a meeting.

_____ 10.   I am afraid to express myself at meetings.

_____ 11.   Communicating at meetings usually makes me uncomfortable.

_____ 12.   I am very relaxed when answering questions at a meeting.

_____ 13.   While participating in a conversation with a new acquaintance, I feel very nervous.

_____ 14.   I have no fear of speaking up in conversations.

_____ 15.   Ordinarily I am very tense and nervous in conversations.

_____ 16.   Ordinarily I am very calm and relaxed in conversations.

_____ 17.   While conversing with a new acquaintance, I feel very relaxed.

_____ 18.   I'm afraid to speak up in conversations.

_____ 19.   I have no fear of giving a speech.

_____ 20. Certain parts of my body feel very tense and rigid while giving a speech.

_____ 21. I feel relaxed while giving a speech.

_____ 22. My thoughts become confused and jumbled when I am giving a speech.

_____ 23. I face the prospect of giving a speech with confidence.

_____ 24. While giving a speech I get so nervous. I forget facts I really know.

Scoring: The PRCA permits computation of one total score and four subscores. The subscores relate to communication apprehension in each of four communication contexts: group discussions, meetings, interpersonal conversations, and public speaking. To compute your scores, merely add or subtract your scores for each item as indicated below.

Subscore Desired	Scoring Formula
Group Discussion	18 + scores for items 2, 4, 6 - scores for 1, 3, 5
Meetings	18 + scores for items 8, 9, 12 - scores for items 7, 10, 11
Interpersonal Conversations	18 + scores for items 14, 16, 17 - scores for items 13, 15, 18
Public Speaking	18 + scores for items 19, 21, 23 - scores for items 20, 22, 24

To obtain your total score for the PRCA, simply add your four subscores together. Your score should range between 24 and 120. If your score is below 24 or above 120, you have made a mistake in computing the score. The lower the score, the greater the communication apprehension.

Discussion: What accounts for communication apprehension? If you scored in the high CA range, what are you afraid might happen if you speak up? As a class, try to identify concrete communicative ways to help someone who is reluctant to speak to feel more comfortable in interactions.

Source: James C. McCroskey. "Measures of Communication-Bound Anxiety." Communication Monographs, 37 (1970): 269-277.

COMMUNICATION IN CONTEXTS

Gender Communication

Family Communication

Multicultural Communication

GENDER ROLES

Goal: To identify the extent to which your behavior reflects a feminine, masculine, or androgynous gender orientation.

Instructions: Each item has three characteristics. Circle the one characteristic of the three that you believe best describes you.

	A	B	C
1.	independent	dependent	interdependent
2.	arumentative	cheerful	moody
3.	active	passive	calm
4.	assertive	affectionate	happy
5.	strong	loyal	unpredictable
6.	analytical	emotional	thoughtful
7.	leader	follower	efficient
8.	self-oriented	other-oriented	sincere
9.	cool	warm	conceited
10.	ambitious	cooperative	adaptable
11.	risky	compassionate	friendly
12.	ambitious	soothing	likeable
13.	opinionated	excitable	conventional
14.	realistic	idealistic	suspicious
15.	brave	gentle	complicated

Total: _____   _____   _____

Interpreting Your Scores: The characteristics associated with column A are masculine; B are feminine; and C are gender-neutral, androgynous, or characteristics consistent with both females and males. The highest score represents your most preferred, pervasive, or in some cases, stereotypical behavioral characteristics. It is likely that your behavioral repertoire includes characteristics from all three. The closer the totals are on each dimension, the more behavioral flexibility you possess; the more discrepant the totals, the more likely you are to display gender rigidity or conformity to gender expectations. Despite your biological sex, it is quite likely that you communicate with more gender diversity than you might imagine.

Discussion: Discussion should surround the idea that biological sex and gender roles are two different things. You may be male, but behave androgynously, for instance. What impact does your gender orientation have on your communication with others? Does androgyny facilitate better communication or understanding between females and males? Does a strict masculine or feminine orientation diminish understanding or impede shared meaning in relationship communication?

SEX-ROLE EXPECTATIONS

Goal: To identify and assess your attitudes about sex roles and sex-role stereotyping.

Instructions: Respond to the statements below using the following scale: 5 = Completely Agree; 4 = Agree; 3 = Neither Agree Nor Disagree; 2 = Disagree; 1 = Completely Disagree. Then form groups of 4-6 persons and discuss each item on the list. Your goal is to reach concensus on each statement or, if that is not possible, to identify areas where significant differences in attitudes exist. Prepare to discuss your group's responses with the class.

_____ 1. Women must work harder than men to be recognized for performing the same task.

_____ 2. Women are more sensitive to relationships than men.

_____ 3. Women and men receive equal pay for equal work.

_____ 4. Men are perceived as more credible than women.

_____ 5. A man is likely to feel uncomfortable if his wife earns a greater salary than him.

_____ 6. A woman is likely to let a man outperform her.

_____ 7. Men are uncomfortable working for a female supervisor.

_____ 8. Women are more emotional than men.

_____ 9. Men are more competitive than women.

_____ 10. Women enjoy being taken care of by a man.

Discussion: Which statements above generate the most concensus in the whole class? Which statements generate the least consensus? Are these generalizations based in biological or social differences? Are generalizations about males and females helpful or a hindrance in your interactions with members of the opposite sex?

GENDER ATTITUDES EXERCISES

Goal: To identify perceptions and attitudes that males and females have of each other.

Exercise 1: "I wish I were a fe/male because . . ."

Complete each of the following statements with the first ideas that come to your mind.

> **Female Responses**: "I am glad I am a female because . . ."
> "I wish I were not a female because . . ."
> "I am glad I am not a male because . . ."
> "I wish I were a male because . . ."

> **Male Responses**: "I am glad I am a male because . . ."
> "I wish I were not a male because . . ."
> "I am glad I am not a female because . . ."
> "I wish I were a female because . . ."

Turn in your answers to your instructor. Do not include your name on this paper, but do indicate whether you are a female or a male. Your instructor will compile the results of the whole classes' responses and try to identify common themes expressed by males and females. A class discussion should focus on perceived advantages and disadvantages of being a member of each sex, on the validity of gender stereotypes, and on whether there does exist an ideal male and female.

Exercise 2: "What really bugs me about fe/males is . . ."

Complete the following two statements: "What really bugs me about females is . . ." "What really bugs me about males is . . ." When you are done, form mixed gender groups and discuss group members' responses. Your discussion should focus on any stereotypes implied by your responses, on communication differences that result from these answers, and on communicative ways for women and men to overcome the effects of these generalizations.

GENDER COMMUNICATION EXERCISE

Goal: To identify female and male communication patterns in relationships.

Instructions:

1. Form same sex groups of four to six persons.

2. Construct a total of <u>ten</u> questions that you want members of the opposite sex to answer. These questions should be related to how males or females communicate in relationships. For instance, why is a woman more likely to self-disclose information about an intimate relationships with her female friends? What do men say to other men about their intimate relationships with women?

3. When you are done, each group member will be responsible for asking at least one question to members of the opposite sex. Volunteers for each side will respond for their group.

Discussion: Did your group have difficulty coming up with questions? Do males and females have fundamentally different or similar interests? Can you identify certain patterns or themes that make communicating with members of the opposite sex frustrating or challenging? Would asking questions like these improve your understanding or communication in female/male relationships?

GENDER-ASSOCIATED CHARACTERISTICS

Male-Associated Characteristics

active
adventurous
aggressive
assertive
autocratic
bossy
capable
coarse
conceited
confident
courageous
cruel
cynical
deliberate
determined
disorderly
dominant
enterprising
forceful
foresighted

frank
greedy
hardheaded
indifferent
individualistic
industrious
initiative
interests wide
inventive
lazy
loud
masculine
obnoxious
opinionated
opportunistic
outspoken
pleasure-seeking
precise
progressive
quick

rational
realistic
reckless
rigid
robust
self-confident
serious
sharp-witted
show-off
shrewd
steady
stern
stingy
stolid
strong
tough
unfriendly
unscrupulous
vindictive
witty

Female-Associated Characteristics

affected
affectionate
appreciative
cautious
changeable
charming
complaining
complicated
confused
considerate
contented
cooperative
curious
dependent
dreamy
emotional
excitable
fault-finding
fearful
feminine

fickle
foolish
forgiving
friendly
frivolous
fussy
gentle
helpful
imaginative
jolly
kind
mild
modest
nervous
patient
pleasant
praising
prudish
self-pitying
sensitive

sentimental
sexy
shy
sincere
soft-hearted
sophisticated
submissive
suggestible
superstitious
sympathetic
talkative
timid
touchy
unambitious
understanding
unintelligent
unstable
warm
weak
worrying

60

WOMEN AND MEN, MEN AND WOMEN

Goal: To encourage empathy, understanding, and respect for what the other gender experiences in interaction.

Instructions:

1. Prior to coming to class, you are to reflect on your experiences in "close" or "intimate" relationships with the other gender. Write down your responses to the following three questions. Then prepare to give a one-minute summary of your answers to the class.

    a. "What responses from the other gender have you most appreciated?"
    b. "How have you known members of your own gender to respond to the other gender in unappreciative or unfair ways?"
    c. "How have members of the other gender responded to you in ways which you didn't appreciate and felt were unfair?"

2. Form groups of 4-6 persons of your <u>same</u> gender. All group members should present summaries for their answer to <u>question "a" only</u>. Your group should reach consensus on the five responses they value most as well as the five responses they think the other gender groups listed as their most valued responses.

3. Form <u>mixed</u> gender groups of 4-6 persons. Each gender should present a summary of his/her priority list to the other group members and then discuss reactions to question "a".

4. Then, rejoin your <u>same</u> gender group to summarize and create a priority list for <u>questions "b" and "c"</u>, similar to what you did above.

5. Then, rejoin your <u>mixed</u> gender group to discuss responses.

6. Finally, the whole class should participate in a discussion of the similarities and differences discovered in women's and men's responses. The focus here should be on generating understanding and respect for the other gender, as well as concrete communicative suggestions for how to bring about this understanding and respect rather than defensiveness, as is common when discussing gender issues.

Discussion: Discussion should center on why there is a tendency for men and women to misunderstand one another, and to become defensive when interaction surrounds gender issues. Is it possible for women and men to really understand one another?

<u>Source</u>: David Lau. "Women and Men, Men and Women." <u>The Speech Communication Teacher</u>, 5 (1991): 9-10.

FAMILY COMMUNICATION RULES

Goal: To identify common rules that determine communication patterns in your family.

Instructions: Answer each of the following questions as they apply to you and your immediate family.

1. Are there any rules for who makes decisions in your family? Are any of these rules related to spending money? household chores? vacations?

2. Are there any rules for determining who speaks to whom in your family? For example, are there rules for what channels of communication are used? for how long parties talk to one another? for how often parties talk to one another?

3. Does everyone have the right to speak freely in your family? Are there any rules which constrain what you say or to whom you say it?

4. Are there any rules that govern how your family interacts during family meals?

5. Are there any rules that determine what you can or cannot say about your family to nonfamily members?

6. Does your family follow any rituals or traditions? What are they and how are they conducted?

7. Can you think of a time when you violated a family rule? What did you do, and what were the repercussions of breaking the rule?

Discussion: Share your answers with the rest of the class. Can you identify common rules that most or all class members have in their families? Why do you suppose that these rules exist? Is it possible to be a member of a family and not have rules to constrain your behavior?

FAMILY COMMUNICATION EXERCISES

Goal: To explore a variety of issues on the relationship between communication and the family.

Instructions: By yourself, answer each of the following questions. Then be prepared to discuss your answers with other members of the class.

1. Name three characteristics of a satisfying family relationship.
   _____
   _____
   _____
   _____

2. What kind of parent do you want to be? How will you communicate with your children?
   _____
   _____
   _____
   _____

3. What are the dominant characteristics of families in our society?
   _____
   _____
   _____
   _____

4. Who should have power and control in the family?
   _____
   _____
   _____
   _____

Discussion: For the first question, discussion should surround the ideal family versus the reality of life in families. For the second, discussion should center on what good family communication skills are and whether more communication is necessarily better in families. For the third, center discussion around multicultural and alternate family lifestyles. For the last, identify the proper balance of power in a family and how that equality might be achieved.

Source: Dr. Valerie McKay, California State University, Long Beach, 1993.

GENDER ASSUMPTIONS IN FAMILIES

Goal: To identify whether your family assigns specific roles to its female and male members, and to identify attitudes about those gender roles in your family.

Instructions:

1. Form groups of 4-6 persons.

2. Your group will be provided with one of the following two scenarios:

   a. "Assume that you are the parents of a 16-year-old who has just obtained a driver's license and wants to date. What rules will you create to govern your child's behavior?"

   b. "Assume you are the parents of a 10-year-old who has the opportunity go to Florida for Spring Break with the family of your child's best friend. What rules will you create to govern your child's behavior?"

3. Your instructor will tell you whether your scenario is designed for a female 16- or 10-year-old, or a male 16- or 10-year-old.

4. Based on the information you are given, generate a list of rules for controlling that child's behavior.

Discussion: Your discussion should identify any rules used to differentiate female children from male children. In addition, do parents have different expectations for their sons and daughters?

Source: Dr. Valeria McKay, California State University, Long Beach, 1993.

COMMUNICATION ADJUSTMENTS TO AGE

Goal: This exercise is designed to demonstrate how one's verbal and nonverbal communication are altered when talking to persons of differing ages.

Instructions: Form groups of 4 persons. Your task is to create a dialogue for the situations given below. This dialogue should reflect a conscious effort to make yourself clearly understood by the recipient of the message; of course, this means that you must adapt your messages to the age of the recipient.

Situations:

1. Explain what clouds and rain are to your 5-year-old brother.

2. Your mother asks you to explain to her how clouds form so that she can relate this information to her 5-year-old son.

3. Tell your 68-year-old grandmother what rap music is and explain to her the meaning of the violence, sex, and obscenity that often appears in rap music videos.

4. You and your best friend (both 19 years old) are discussing the violence, sex, and obscenity that appear in a recent MTV rap video. You friend asks for your opinion on this music.

5. Your sister is 13 years old. She asks you to tell her what sex is. What are you going to say?

6. Your brother is 5 years old. He ask you to tell him where babies come from. What are you going to say?

7. Your father allowed you to borrow his new sports car for your date on Saturday night. On Sunday, he wants an explanation for how and why his car's back bumper is dented.

8. Your 18-year-old sister wants an explanation for the dented bumper on Dad's new sports car.

Discussion: Class discussion should surround the idea that our verbal and nonverbal choices are affected by the age, life experience, cognitive ability, and language comprehension of the listener. Identify specific verbal and nonverbal elements you alter when speaking to someone much older and younger than yourself. Also identify specific strategies used to make yourself understood to someone who doesn't share your frame of reference or typical language use. Are there any messages that do not have to be altered because of age differences?

DON'T JUDGE A BOOK BY ITS COVER

Goal: To become aware of the advantages of suspending judgments in cross-cultural communication settings.

Instructions:

1. On a piece of paper, answer the following questions:

    a.   What is your favorite color?
    b.   What is your favorite food?
    c.   What is your favorite type of music?
    d.   What city in the United States would you like to visit?
    e.   What country in the world would you like to visit?
    f.   What is your favorite hobby?
    g.   What is your favorite pasttime?
    h.   What is your favorite sport?

2. When you have completed your answers, your instructor will pair you with another member of the class. Your instructor will make a conscious effort to pair you up with someone who appears physically to be different from you (i.e., male with female, black student with white student, muscular student with petite student, etc.).

3. Without engaging in any form of verbal or nonverbal interaction with your partner, answer all questions above about your partner. When you have finished, then read aloud your responses to your partner, and verify their accuracy or inaccuracy. Total the number of your correct responses.

Discussion: Discussion should center on the problems of judging a person by racial, cultural, physical, or gender related stereotypes. Did you find that you actually have more similarities than differences with your partner? How easy was it to answer the questions, even in the absence of any information about your partner?

Source: Gail Armstead Hankins. "Don't Judge a Book by Its Cover." Speech Communication Teacher, 5 (1991): 8.

AMERICAN CULTURAL VALUES

The following characteristics typify American cultural values, attitudes, and assumptions. For comparison purposes, the values, attitudes, and assumptions in opposition to these American cultural orientations are also listed.

American Value	Value Opposition
1. doing	1. being
2. external achievement	2. spontaneous expression
3. optimistic	3. fatalistic
4. fast, busy pace of life	4. steady, rhythmic pace
5. stress means of achievement	5. stress final goals
6. material goals in life	6. spiritual goals in life
7. desire pleasure and absence of pain	7. experience fullness of pleasure and pain
8. individual responsibility	8. group responsibility
9. pragmatic orientation	9. ideal orientation
10. active learning	10. passive, rote learning
11. flexible roles	11. rigid roles
12. stress equality	12. stress hierarchy
13. stress informality	13. stress formality
14. sexual equality	14. male superiority
15. task-centered	15. people-centered
16. social friendships	16. intense friendships
17. friends are shared	17. friends are exclusive
18. nonbinding relationships	18. binding relationships
19. interaction is fun	19. interaction is proper
20. individualistic	20. conforming to roles
21. world is physical	21. world is spiritual
22. world is rational	22. world is mystical
23. people are apart from nature	23. people are part of nature
24. nature is changeable	24. nature is permanent
25. truth is relative	25. truth is absolute
26. future is important	26. past is important
27. time is linear	27. time is circular
28. private ownership	28. public use
29. self-reliance	29. reliance on authority
30. self-identity	30. group identity
31. youth is valued	31. experience is valued
32. social control is achieved through persuasion	32. social control is achieved through guilt and shame
33. inductive problem-solving	33. transdeductive
34. judgments by comparison	34. judgments by absolute standards

TOLERANCE FOR HUMAN DIVERSITY
(THDI 50)

Goal: To examine how your attitudes toward various groups of citizens within the United States influence your communication choices.

Instructions: This questionnaire was designed to help explore attitudes toward various groups of citizens within the United States. Please read each question and mark the answer which most closely describes your feelings. It is important that you mark the questions as truthfully as possible. Giving the socially acceptable answer rather than the answer that most accurately describes how you feel causes problems in the interpretation of the scores, so please answer as accurately as possible. <u>Please mark all answers on the answer sheet provided</u>.

<u>How often do you interact with people in the following categories?</u> <u>Use the following key</u>: A = constantly; B = frequently; C = regularly; D = occasionally; E = never.

1. Handicapped/disabled/differently abled.
2. Someone racially different from yourself.
3. Someone who belongs to different faith/religion/denomination than your own.
4. Someone a generation older than yourself.
5. Someone a generation younger than yourself.
6. Someone belonging to a socioeconomic level that is different from your own.
7. Someone whose sexual orientation is different from your own.
8. Someone of the opposite gender.

<u>For the next group of items, use the following key:</u> A = Strongly Agree; B = Agree; C = Disagree; D = Strongly Disagree.

9. Diversity among American citizens is what makes this country strong.
10. A handicapped person can be as good an employee as an abled person.
11. I would not marry a person of a different race/ethnicity.
12. America would be a better place if men and women stuck to their assigned roles.
13. I feel anxious when I talk with members of the opposite sex.
14. I would not be roommates with a person of a different race/ethnicity.
15. People who are poor just don't want to work.
16. I feel comfortable in a group of people where I am in the racial minority.
17. America would be a better place if we deported all of the gay people.
18. I would not be ashamed to admit that one of my family members was gay.
19. I feel nervous when I see or have to interact with a person who is differently abled either mentally or physically.
20. I would go to church with friends of mine who belonged to a faith/religion/denomination that was different from my own.
21. I would not object to having housing for the poor in my neighborhood.
22. There is only one true religion/faith.
23. Most jobs can be done effectively regardless of the gender of the worker.
24. Both men and women are equally trustworthy.
25. Children should be seen and not heard.
26. Public buildings should be made accessible to the handicapped.
27. In America many people are poor due to situations beyond their control.

28. American unity is not as high as it should be because of the many differences in race, language, and religion of its citizens.
29. I would not be ashamed to admit that a person in my family belonged to a different race/ethnicity.
30. People of religions/faiths/denominations different from mine often have practices that are questionable or strange.
31. I feel comfortable around people must older than me.
32. People who suffer from mental retardation are of little benefit to society.
33. I would not hesitate to date a person of a different race/ethnicity.
34. If a hearing impaired person can speak, s/he should not use sign language in the presence of people who can hear.
35. I would be comfortable at gatherings where a majority of the people were gay.
36. People of the opposite gender have too many irritating habits and manners.
37. Monetary wealth and material possessions are the most important indicators of how successful a person is.
38. I feel anxious around people much younger than me.
39. I feel comfortable attending church with a group of people whose religion/faith/denomination is different from mine.
40. Talking and interacting with people who have much more or much less money than I do does not cause me anxiety.
41. People of the opposite gender are more similar than different to me.
42. Old people have too many irritating habits and manners.
43. A gay couple would be allowed in my home.
44. America would be a better place if everyone belonged to the same religion/faith/denomination.
45. Talking to little children can be interesting.
46. Americans who remain loyal to their own subculture can be equally as loyal to the United States as a whole.
47. People should be forced to retire at a certain age.
48. America would be a stronger country if there was more tolerance for differences among its citizens.
49. If I know a person is homosexual, I restrict my interactions with her/him.
50. Diversity among U.S. citizens is what has weakened the fabric of this country.

Which of these categories would you use to describe yourself? Mark A (yes) if the descriptor fits you. Mark B (no) if it does not. It is important that you mark each choice A or B!

Ethnic Heritage
51. African American 52. Asian American/Pacific Islander
53. European American 54. Latino/Hispanic/Chicano
55. Native American 56. Interethnic/Interracial
57. International or Other

Gender 58. Female 59. Male

Economic Status 60. Upper Income 61. Middle Income
62. Lower Income

Religion	63.	Protestant	64.	Catholic	65.	Baptist
	66.	Methodist	67.	Presbyterian	68.	Episcopalian
	69.	Lutheran	70.	Morman	71.	Evangelical
	72.	Pentecostal	73.	Christian	74.	Jewish
	75.	Moslem	76.	Buddhist	77.	Hindu
	78.	Agnostic	79.	Atheist	80.	Other

Answer Sheet for Tolerance for Human Diversity Inventory--TCDI 50

1. ____	21. ____	41. ____	61. ____
2. ____	22. ____	42. ____	62. ____
3. ____	23. ____	43. ____	63. ____
4. ____	24. ____	44. ____	64. ____
5. ____	25. ____	45. ____	65. ____
6. ____	26. ____	46. ____	66. ____
7. ____	27. ____	47. ____	67. ____
8. ____	28. ____	48. ____	68. ____
9. ____	29. ____	49. ____	69. ____
10. ____	30. ____	50. ____	70. ____
11. ____	31. ____	51. ____	71. ____
12. ____	32. ____	52. ____	72. ____
13. ____	33. ____	53. ____	73. ____
14. ____	34. ____	54. ____	74. ____
15. ____	35. ____	55. ____	75. ____
16. ____	36. ____	56. ____	76. ____
17. ____	37. ____	57. ____	77. ____
18. ____	38. ____	58. ____	78. ____
19. ____	39. ____	59. ____	79. ____
20. ____	40. ____	60. ____	80. ____

Scoring the Tolerance for Human Diversity Inventory

1. The following questions, Patterns of Interaction 1 - 8, should be scored: A = 5, B = 4, C = 3, D = 2, E = 1. Add 1 - 8 with scores ranging from 8 - 40. On a normal curve with 6 stanines, the range would be as follows: High = 28 - 40; Moderate = 13 - 27; Low = 0 - 12.

2. The following questions which are positive--9, 10, 16, 18, 20, 21, 23, 24, 26, 27, 29, 31, 33, 35, 39, 40, 41, 43, 45, 46, 48--should be scored as follows: A = 4, B = 3, C = 2, D = 1.

3. The following questions which are negative--11, 12, 13, 14, 15, 17, 19, 22, 25, 28, 30, 32, 34, 36, 37, 38, 42, 44, 47, 49, 50--should be scored as follows: A = 1, B = 2, C = 3, D = 4.

4. Add 9 - 50 with scores ranging from 42 - 168. On a normal shaped curve with 3 stanines above and 3 stanines below the mean, the scores would be interpreted as follows: High = 113 - 168; Moderate = 57 - 112; Low = 42 - 56.

Source: Marquita L. Byrd. The Intracultural Communication Book. New York: McGraw-Hill, 1993, pp. 192-197.

AN EXERCISE ON DIVERSITY

Goal: To provide a means by which you can apply effective communication skills in situations dealing with ethnic differences, develop a greater sense of awareness of who you are, and a better understanding of those around you.

Instructions: Nearly everyday we hear of ethnic and racial conflicts occurring in different parts of our country, resulting from misunderstandings and ineffective communication. Though diversity may be one of our nation's greatest strengths, it may also lead to our downfall. As roles change and the nation becomes more integrated, the possibility of ethnic strife increases. Recent events in Los Angeles illustrate well the chaos resulting from the neglect of these issues. It is essential that all groups in our country learn to understand and effectively communicate with each other if we are to succeed as a society. The following exercise is designed to serve as a good catalyst for thoughtful and enlightened classroom discussion.

1. **Write** a 1 - 2 page paper that answers the following questions:

   a. What is your nationality, ethnic background, or group identification? (You may define "group" any way you like.)
   b. How strong of a tie to this group do you feel?
   c. How is this tie manifested? Are ethnic traditions in the family maintained in such areas as food, dress, language, travel, work, rituals on holidays, roles played by family members, etc.?
   d. Was your group in the majority or minority where you grew up? Were ethnic traditions maintained in your neighborhood?
   e. Were there other groups in your neighborhood? How did you feel about those groups?
   f. What are some of the stereotypes others assigned to your group?
   g. Have you ever felt discriminated against because of your association with a group? Give examples.
   h. What do you think needs to be done to create better understanding among different groups in our school, state, and nation?

2. Bring your paper to the next class meeting (see next page for examples of papers). Form groups of 4 - 5 persons and share your paper with them. Be prepared to discuss your experiences with the class as a whole.

Examples:

Sean: I am 3/4 Irish and 1/4 German. I feel a very strong tie to the Irish in me but not really any tie to the German. I was raised in a very Irish-Catholic home. I've been to Ireland twice in the last five years. We do a log of traditional Irish things on birthdays, holidays, weddings, etc. I grew up in a neighborhood that was mostly Irish. My father was a policeman. I went to a Catholic school. Some of the stereotypes associated with the Irish are they they are potatoeaters, pig headed, hot tempered, and drinkers. I've never experienced discrimination. We had some minority kids at our school and kids would make fun of them. A black family moved into our neighborhood and they were driven out. To avoid prejudice, people must keep an open mind.

Maya: My nationality is African-American and I feel strong emotional and physical ties to this group. I feel strong ties because of the history of my ethnic group. Unfortunately, there are a number of stereotypes: (1) laxiness; (2) we are products of years of living on welfare; (3) we are ignorant and illiterate; (4) the men are weak and the women are strong and domineering and keep the family going; (5) we only wash our hair once a year; (6) we are athletic and always excel in sports; (7) we can't control our sex drives. I have personally been discriminated against several times. Once I applied for a job and on the phone the manager said I was what she was looking for and so arranged for an interview. When I arrived she said that I didn't look the way I sounded and that the company already had their quota of blacks. I think to stop stereotypes the government should incorporate mandatory classes that deal with and discuss minority issues and can address these myths and stereotypes. Only after learning about each other will we begin to respect each other.

Helga: My ethnic background is German but I have no ties to it. I come from an all white rural town that is very prejudiced to non-whites like blacks, hispanics, and so on. The group I come from is considered "hicks." It's not really fair to call me a "hick" just like it's not fair to call someone else a stereotypical name. . . .

Discussion: As a class, you should try to identify common themes among those who have and have not experienced prejudice, those who and do not feel strong ties to their ethnic heritage, and what accounts for discrimination or the lack thereof. Pay particular attention to question H on the previous page. In other words, try to generate concrete communicative ways to validate others and simultaneously minimize prejudice and stereotypes.

Source: Ken Hawkinson. "Two Exercises on Diversity and Gender." The Speech Communication Teacher, 8 (1993): 2-4.

STATUS AND MULTICULTURAL COMMUNICATION

Goal: The purpose of this exercise is to demonstrate that different value and status is accorded to persons based on their cultural background.

Instructions: Prepare to role-play the following encounters. In doing so, try to imagine what each person's attitude and appearance would likely be prior to the encounter. Then construct dialogue that you envision would likely occur in this situation.

1. A young black man faces a judge in traffic court for having run a red light.

2. A white elderly woman faces a judge in traffic court for having run a red light.

3. An Hispanic woman asks a professor for an extension on a term paper.

4. A male football player asks a professor for an extension on a term paper.

5. A native Vietnamese woman orders a hamburger in a small restaurant.

6. A young black woman orders a hamburger in a small restaurant.

7. A white male businessman makes an appointment with a busy doctor or lawyer.

8. A young Hispanic man makes an appointment with a busy doctor or lawyer.

Discussion: Each role-play should be discussed and analyzed in terms of what behavioral differences the participant displayed and how cultural origin influences attitudes and behaviors in typical situations like these.

TEACHING CHILDREN

Goal: To examine different culturally-based values by identifying what values children should possess.

Instructions: Answer each of the questions below with a "yes" or "no" response. Then join a group of 4 - 6 persons and try to arrive at consensus about how to answer each question. Be prepared to inform the class of your group's results.

Yes   **No**

___ ___ 1. It is more important to teach children to be independent than to be obligated to parents or others.

___ ___ 2. It is more important for children to appreciate nature than to control the environment.

___ ___ 3. It is more important for children to appreciate what they have than to strive for a better life.

___ ___ 4. It is more important for children to be cooperative than competitive.

___ ___ 5. It is more important for children to be creative than to be useful.

___ ___ 6. It is more important for children to have a few deep friendships than to be able to relate to many persons.

___ ___ 7. It is more important for children to develop sensitivity to others than to openly confront conflicts with others.

___ ___ 8. It is more important for children to learn discipline and rules than to develop creative imaginations.

___ ___ 9. Unconditional acceptance is more important than strict discipline in bringing up children.

___ ___ 10. It is more important for children to believe that all people are equal than that certain persons should enjoy special status because of their age, family role, or profession.

Discussion: Discussion should center on the fact thatt both options in each statement have desirable qualities. Given that there is no right or wrong answer, to what degree is each statement determined by cultural background? Is your choice based on individual preferences without regard to cultural values? Are any of these statements determined by gender differences? Is there an American cultural pattern in these statements?

STEREOTYPING

Goal: To identify and evaluate the stereotypes you hold.

Instructions:

1.   You will form groups of 4-6 persons and conduct a panel discussion in front of the class on one of the following topics. Each group member should briefly summarize her/his position on the topic. After each member has spoken, the discussion will be opened up to the other panel members and eventually to the class as a whole.

2.   **Topics**:

   a.   How is the A through F grading system used widely in schools related to stereotyping?

   b.   Identify a specific stereotype about a religious, ethnic, or political group. Explain how your stereotypes developed and how it influences your behavior toward that group.

   c.   Generate a list of attitudes you have held, or still hold, that you consider to be stereotypes. In what way can they be perceived as stereotypes?

Discussion: Discussion should surround the following: Is it possible to behave toward any person without relying on stereotypes to some degree? Is it hard to admit to having stereotypes? Are you afraid to say something because it might be construed as stereotypic or biased? To what degree did the presence of the class affect what you said during the discussion?   Why did this make a difference?

MULTICULTURAL INTERVIEW

Goal: To appreciate cultural diversity and to identify communication similarities and differences in a specific culture.

Instructions: You are to interview someone who is a member of a culture different than yours. Cultures include national, ethnic, racial, color, generational, or sexual. When you have completed your interview, answer all of the questions below. Then be prepared to discuss your interview in class and to turn in a written summary of your interview.

1. What is the nature of the interviewee's culture? Include this individual's ethnicity, co-culture, age, gender, place of origin (if not the United States), and length of residency in the United States (if relevant).

2. How do you think others outside of your co-culture perceive you? Does this perception differ from how you perceive yourself?

3. What are the misconceptions and stereotypes you have had to cope with or counteract when interacting with members of your interviewee's co-culture?

4. What values are accepted by your interviewee? These values may include family, religion, aspirations, sex roles, etc. Do these values differ from your own culture or the mainstream culture?

5. What contributions does your interviewee's co-culture make to the mainstream society?

6. Is your interviewee satisfied with the status currently held of her/his co-culture in the United States? Are you satisfied? If not, how would you ideally like it to be?

7. What insights have you gained as a result of this interview?

Discussion: Each individual in the class should summarize the major communicative insights gained from this interview experience. In addition, the class should identify common themes, common stereotypes, or potential sources of multicultural conflict. Finally, the class should generate communicative ways to manage multicultural differences.

PATTERNS OF COMMUNICATION

Communication Rules

Listening

Assertiveness

Self-Disclosure

Conflict

COMMUNICATION RULES EXERCISE

Goal: To identify the pervasiveness of rules in virtually all communication contexts.

Instructions:

1. Choose one of the following common contexts in which you are likely to find yourself (or identify your own context to examine):

   a. party-going behavior
   b. beach-going behavior
   c. dating behavior
   d. restaurant-eating behavior
   e. shopping mall behavior
   f. car-buying behavior
   g. family get-together behavior
   h. Christmas morning behavior
   i. wedding rituals
   j. movie-going behavior
   k. football spectator behavior

2. Generate a list of rules which governs your behavior in the above contexts. That is, how are you expected to act? And, what is likely to happen if you violate those rules or expectations?

3. What can you **not** do in these contexts? In other words, what are you prohibited from doing or saying?

4. In addition, try to identify the origin of those rules. In other words, **why** do these rules exist? What is their logic or rationale?

Discussion: Discussion of this exercise should surround the pervasiveness and potency of rules, the role that conformity and uncertainty reduction play with respect to rules, how rules can be changed, and how communication is constrained and evaluated on the basis of rules.

VIOLATING COMMUNICATION RULES

Goal: The purpose of this exercise is to help you identify the norms of communication by violating those norms.

Instructions: Choose one of the scenarios below to enact. Pair up with a classmate and have one person engage in the violation of the rule while the other observes reactions to the violation.

1. Engage someone in conversation for five minutes. Assume that whatever the other party says is a lie. Respond accordingly.

2. Begin a conversation with a friend or acquaintance. Respond to each statement the other party makes with a question of clarification, a request for elaboration, or a paraphrase. In other words, don't make any assumptions or any indications that you understand what the other person means.

3. Engage one of your parents or siblings in a conversation for five minutes, but assume that you know nothing about this person. In other words, treat this family member as a complete stranger.

4. Enter an elevator full of strangers. When the doors close, begin to talk to them.

5. Walk up to a stranger and, without saying a word, invade her/his space. In other words, stand too close to the other without justifying or apologizing for the invasion.

Discussion: How did you feel violating a communication rule? What rule did you actually violate? How did others respond to your violation? What were the negative and/or positive consequences of this violation?

PRIORITIES IN LISTENING

Goal: To identify the skills you believe are most important in listening.

Instructions: Rank order the following list by placing a 1 next to the behavior you find the single most important component of listening. Mark a 2 for the second most important in listening and so on. When you are done, form groups of 4-6 persons and arrive at concensus about the priority of these listening skills. Be prepared to discuss your group's rank order with the class.

_____   Do not interrupt a speaker.

_____   Pay full attention to the speaker.

_____   Give feedback to the speaker.

_____   Make a speaker feel that her/his message is important.

_____   Make sure that the speaker's message is accurate and error-free.

_____   Do not rush a speaker.

_____   Do not judge or evaluate a speaker's message.

_____   Make sure you prepare a response to the speaker's message.

_____   Allow a speaker to deliver a message at his/her pace without rushing or becoming impatient with the speaker.

_____   Insure that the speaker knows you can be trusted to keep information confidential.

Discussion: Which is more important: the accuracy of the message or confirming the person speaking? What is the relationship between what is said and what is meant? How can you avoid judging while listening?

LISTENING HABITS

Poor Listening

1. <u>Our Minds Won't Wait</u>: Our thoughts can race along from four to ten times faster than most people speak. So, while we are waiting for the words to come in, the mind tunes out, then in again. The result: only a few words penetrate, and we miss the whole point.
2. <u>We Think We Know Already</u>: And so we listen with just "half an ear."
3. <u>We're Looking, Not Listening</u>: How often in introductions has a name failed to penetrate because your mind was occupied with its owner's appearance or mannerisms?
4. <u>We Are Busy Listeners</u>: We try to listen while giving part of our attention to a newspaper, radio, or television program.
5. <u>We Miss The Big Ideas</u>: We're listening to words, not ideas. We take words at face value rather than looking beyond the words to the ideas expressed or the relationship level emphasized.
6. <u>Our Emotions Make Us Deaf</u>: We take innocent comments as personal attacks, or, when someone offers opposing ideas on a matter about which we have a strong opinion, we unconsciously feel that it is risky to listen because we might hear something that could make us question our own views. We mentally stop receiving while we plan our verbal counterattack.
7. <u>We Ambush</u>: We listen carefully, but only to collect information to use to attack what the other person has said. The prosecuting attorney syndrome.
8. <u>We Interrupt Too Much</u>: You cannot listen if you are interrupting.

Good Listening

1. <u>Stop Talking</u>: This includes the silent debating, retorting, and rehearsing that goes on in the mind.
2. <u>React Appropriately</u>: Give positive or negative feedback that shows you agree, disagree, etc. Also, look attentive nonverbally. You'll listen better if you look like you're listening.
3. <u>Concentrate On What Is Being Said</u>: Attend to words, ideas, and feelings. Put the speaker's ideas into your own words to generate understanding.
4. <u>Get Rid Of Distractions</u>: Avoid props, doodling, phone calls, the television, etc.
5. <u>Don't Give Up Too Soon</u>: Don't interrupt or be too quick to respond.
6. <u>Avoid Making Assumptions</u>: If you disagree, don't assume the person is uninformed, lying, dumb, etc.
7. <u>Don't Argue Mentally</u>: Control your anger, give the other a fair hearing.
8. <u>Share Responsibility For The Communication</u>: Remember that what occurs communicatively is the result of both parties; no one party is entirely to blame.
9. <u>Ask Questions</u>: Be active, don't assume that you really understand what another is saying. Ask to make sure.
10. <u>Paraphrase</u>: Restate what you think the other just said in your own words and request feedback that you interpreted the other accurately.

LISTENING FOR FEELINGS

Goal: To identify the effects of good and poor listening on another's feelings.

Instructions: Confirming or disconfirming behavior is related to what you do in your listening. When you do not listen to others, you do not hear their words; you also--and this is very important--tell them something of your attitude about them as persons. Role-play the following situations in which you make up dialogue and action to suit what you think would happen. Concentrate as you do this on the effect your listening behavior would have on the feelings the other persons might have about themselves, about you, and about how you value each other as persons--not only on how you hear the words spoken.

1. **Situation**: Three people are discussing a movie. Select a movie which all members of the group have seen. One person should attempt to fill in the plot, cast of characters, etc., while another listens and helps. The third person should pay no attention to the "data" or information being presented but should only watch for errors in grammar, vocalized pauses, mispronunciations, or other personal slips by the speakers--including just plain ignoring the topic, mentioning people passing by, or relating other events outside the topic of the movie. At the end of the role playing, ask the class and members of the group to react to how they feel about the "disconfirmer." What should have been done to make a more effective communication situation?

2. **Situation**: A family is having dinner--two parents, three children. All the children attend school. The youngest wants to tell about something that happened today. None of the others pay attention but instead interrupt to have food passed or to laugh at a joke they heard on television, somehow managing to keep the speaker from ever getting reinforcement to tell the story.

3. **Situation**: A planning group in class is getting ready to speak on an assigned topic. One member continually makes suggestions which "plop" or never get acknowledged by the others. Later, when another member suggests the same thing, it may get picked up. Indicate in the role playing how silence toward a participant can make such a person give up membership in the group. Listening can be a supportive activity on a personal level, or it can be a device to extinguish another person in a group.

4. **Situation**: A lecturer in front of an audience is met by a variety of listening behaviors. Role-play the kinds of listening which can take place and make use of "alter egos" (or persons speaking for the actors as if they were speaking their thoughts) to show what is happening in the listener and how that shows up in overt behavior.

Discussion: Discussion should surround what happens to the quality of communication under each of the above conditions, how the speaker feels, what is attributed to those who are not listening, what consequences listening (or lack thereof) has on the relationships between participants, and what concrete communicative skills could be used to improve each of the role-plays.

Source: Gail E. Myers, and Michele Tolela Myers. The Dynamics of Human Communication: A Laboratory Approach, 6th ed. New York: McGraw-Hill, 1992, pp. 447-448.

LISTENING EXERCISES

Goal: To identify elements of good and poor listening, and to recognize barriers that impede quality listening.

Instructions: One or both of these activities will be done in class prior to talking about the topic of listening.

Exercise 1: Your instructor will ask for four volunteers to write down ten unrelated words on a piece of paper. These volunteers will then participate in a role-play in front of the class. This simulated situation involved four persons: Daughter and Boyfriend discuss their marriage plans with her Mom and Dad who are opposed to the marriage. As Mom, Dad, Daughter, and Boyfriend converse, they must fit their ten words into the discussion <u>in the order</u> written on their paper. After all of the words have been used, the instructor will collect the cards and then ask Mom to name the words on Dad's paper, Dad to name the words on Daughter's paper, Daughter to name the words on Boyfriend's paper, and Boyfriend to name the words on Mom's paper. Chances are that they will not be able to name more than 2 or 3 words, so when they are done, the rest of the class can help to name the rest of the words. The audience is usually much more proficient in naming the words than the participants in the role-play.

Exercise 2: Your instructor will ask for five volunteers. Four of the five will leave the room and wait to be called back inside. The remaining volunteer in the classroom will listen as the instructor reads a "farm story." At the completion of the story, the first volunteer will call in one of the persons standing outside and relate the farm story to him/her. The second volunteer then will relate her/his version of the story to the third volunteer who is brought back into the classroom. Continue this until all participants have been told the story. Your teacher will instruct the rest of the class members to listen carefully to all five stories and record omissions, distortions, and additions as they occur.

Discussion: Discussion for the first exercise should surround the fact that those involved in interactions are too busy thinking of what they are going to say next to listen attentively to what the others have to say. This should lead to a class discussion of barriers to effective listening. For the second exercise, discussion should focus on what information was added to the story, what was lost, whether the information was presented in the correct sequence, where in the sequence did most of the information get lost, and what might have been done to improve the communication effort. On the basis of both exercises, what constitutes good listening? poor listening? How can one become a better listener? How can a speaker help a listener to attend and comprehend more efficiently and effectively?

Note: The "farm story" can be found in the Appendix at the end of the workbook.

A BILL OF ASSERTIVE RIGHTS

People often avoid conflicts because they see no options other than avoidance. They are afraid to assert themselves or "engage" others in conflict because they have so much uncertainty about the outcomes. The following list comes from the book <u>When I Say No, I Feel Guilty</u> by Manuel J. Smith, and is useful for determining whether you are locked into an unproductive personal conflict style, or whether you have a pattern of unassertiveness.

1. You have the right to judge your own behavior, thoughts, and emotions, and to take the responsibility for their initiation and consequences upon yourself.

2. You have the right to offer no reasons or excuses for justifying your behavior.

3. You have the right to judge if you are responsible for finding solutions to other people's problems.

4. You have the right to change your mind.

5. You have the right to make mistakes--and be responsible for them.

6. You have the right to say "I don't know."

7. You have the right to be independent of the goodwill of others before coping with them.

8. You have the right to say "I don't understand."

9. You have the right to be illogical in making decisions.

10. You have the right to say "I don't care."

Source: Manuel J. Smith. <u>When I Say No, I Feel Guilty</u>. New York: The Dial Press, 1975.

ASSERTIVENESS COMPARISON

Goal: This comparison and contrast among persons who are nonassertive, assertive, and aggressive is designed for you to discover the styles that best fit your own behavior.

	Nonassertive	Directly Aggressive	Indirectly Aggressive	Assertive
Approach to Others	I'm not OK, You're OK.	I'm OK, You're not OK.	I'm OK, You're not OK (but I'll let you think you are).	I'm OK, You're OK.
Decision Making	Let others choose.	Choose for others. They know it.	Choose for others. They don't know it.	Chooses for self.
Self-Sufficiency	Low	High or Low	Looks high but usually low	Usually high
Behavior in Problem Situations	Flees, gives in	Outright attack	Concealed attack	Direct confrontation
Response of Others	Disrespect, guilt, anger, frustration	Hurt, defensiveness, humiliation	Confusion, frustration, feelings of manipulation	Mutual respect
Success Pattern	Succeeds by luck or charity of others	Beats out others	Wins by manipulation	Attempts "win-win" or "no-lose" solutions

Source: S. Phelps, and N. Austin. *The Assertive Woman*. San Luis Obispo, CA: Impact, 1974, p. 11.

ASSERTION, NONASSERTION, AND AGGRESSION

Goal: The purpose of this exercise is to distinguish among assertive, nonassertive, and aggressive responses.

Instructions: Form groups of 4-6 persons and construct an assertive, nonassertive, and aggressive response for each of the ten situations below.

1. A teenager cuts in front of you while you wait in line at the post office.

2. A group you are talking with calls your friend Debra a "nigger." You are offended.

3. Your communication teacher keeps giving you low grades on your speeches. You think this is unfair.

4. You are the only one who doesn't want to go to dinner at the restaurant your three friends have chosen.

5. Your parents object to the person you are dating. They are planning a birthday party for you and have not invited your significant other.

6. You would like to meet the family who has just moved into the house across the street from you.

7. The couple behind you at the movie theatre will not stop talking.

8. You see your friend cheating during the midterm examination in the biology class you are both taking.

9. You are driving in the fast lane on the freeway and become irritated with the driver in front of you because s/he is going only 55 mph.

10. Your friend compliments you on your new designer haircut.

Discussion: Discussion should surround whether you can identify with one kind of response versus another. In other words, are you more likely to respond aggressively, assertively, or nonassertively? Which responses were hardest to construct? Which were easiest? Which situations were conducive to assertive responses? What factors (i.e., familiarity with the person, importance of the issue) influenced your choice to respond assertively or nonassertively rather than aggressively?

ASSERTIVENESS INVENTORY

Goal: The purpose of this exercise is to help you identify some important forms of communication that you may wish to improve through learning the skills of assertiveness.

Instructions: For each of the scenarios below, indicate the degree to which you would be <u>satisfied</u> with how you would act using the following scale:

Scale:
    5 = Completely satisfied with how I would act.
    4 = Probably, but not totally satisfied, with how I would act.
    3 = Neither satisfied nor dissatisfied with how I would act.
    2 = Probably, but not totally dissatisfied with how I would act.
    1 = Completely dissatisfied with how I would act.

____ 1.   You are on an airplane, sitting next to a person who seems friendly and begins a conversation with you.

____ 2.   You are attending a birthday party of one of your friends. You don't know many of the people attending the party, but you would like to be social and have a good time.

____ 3.   You have not yet met your new next door neighbors. You are watering your front yard when this family pulls up in their driveway.

____ 4.   Your good friend just bought a new outfit that you think looks awful. Your friend asks for your opinion.

____ 5.   You didn't understand much of your teacher's lecture and have a lot of questions, but everyone else in the class seems to have understood the lecture.

____ 6.   The conflict you had with your friend disturbs you because you realize you were wrong. You know you need to apologize to your friend. You and your friend are now sitting next to one another before class starts.

____ 7.   Your boss just accused you of being lazy on the job.

____ 8.   Your friend has left numerous messages on your telephone answering machine. You haven't returned your friend's calls because you have been busy. Now, you have run into your friend who accuses you of not caring anymore.

____ 9.   You are concerned about your mother who has been moody lately. When you ask what is wrong, she tells you to mind your own business.

____ 10. You are irritated with your girl/boyfriend because s/he is always late. You hoped that this feeling would go away in time but it has not, and now you feel resentful.

_____ 11. You have waited for more than 20 minutes to be seated at a restaurant. Patrons who have come in after you have already been seated.

_____ 12. Your next door neighbors have five cars. Most of the time, at least one of these cars is partially blocking your driveway.

_____ 13. You have been invited to a party by your friend. Your friend already knows that you don't have plans for that evening, but you don't want to go to this party.

_____ 14. You have been assigned to be leader of your class group. You want to delegate responsibilities to each group member, but you don't want to sound bossy.

_____ 15. Your classmate asks to borrow your notes because s/he missed the lecture again. You have done this in the past for other classmates and have never received your notes back from these other persons.

Assessing Your Scores: The above questions relate to the following assertiveness skills: 1-3 are conversation skills; 4-6 are expressing feelings; 7-9 are handling criticism, 10-12 are managing conflicts, and 13-15 are saying "no" and making requests. For most of us, assertiveness is situationally-bound. That is, we may have no problems expressing feelings, but are anxious about saying "no." Consequently, one way to assess your assertiveness skills is to add up the scores for each of the five areas separately. The lower your score in that area, the more you need to work on improving your assertiveness. For each category, a score below 6 suggests that you need to work on this skill, while a score over 12 indicates that you have no problems asserting yourself on this dimension. If you total all of your scores together, you will get an indication of your general level of satisfaction with your assertiveness skills. A score above 60 suggests considerable satisfaction with your assertiveness skills overall whereas a score below 30 suggests that you need to work on your ability to assert yourself in a number of contexts.

JOHARI WINDOW EXERCISES

Goal: The purpose of these exercises is to identify the openness of your communication, and to reinforce the importance of self-disclosure and feedback to self-awareness.

Instructions: The Johari Window provides a way to look at your "self" and how aware you are of information about yourself. According to the Johari Window, quality interpersonal communication and rewarding relationships are predicated on increasing the size of the "open" or "public" area. This can only be accomplished through self-disclosure and soliciting feedback from others. The following are four aspects or "quadrants" of information about the self.

1. <u>Area 1</u>: represents your <u>open</u> area. The information is common knowledge and you feel free about sharing that information with others.

2. <u>Area 2</u>: represents your <u>blind</u> area, information others have about you, but that you do not have. This is the way you look to other people.

3. <u>Area 3</u>: represents your <u>hidden</u> area, things that you know about yourself but have been unwilling to share with others. This area includes your secrets and things about which you are ashamed.

4. <u>Area 4</u>: represents your <u>unknown</u> area, things about you which you don't understand. This is the area of needs, expectations, desires that you have which you cannot consciously comprehend.

The four areas are interdependent. Any change in the size of one area affects the size of the others. Self-disclosure increases the size of the open area and decreases the size of the hidden area. Requesting constructive feedback from others increases the size of the open area and decreases the size of the blind area. Thus, the Johari Window can aid you in generating more understanding of the self.

On the following pages are a series of exercises to create awareness of yourself in relation to others.

1. Draw a Johari Window for each of the following relationships: your mother, your father, your girl/boyfriend, your boss, and your best friend.

Free Self	Blind Self
Hidden Self	Unknown Self

2. Make a list of _five_ things that you know about yourself that you are sure others also know about you (open area).

3. Make a list of _five_ things that you know about yourself that you are fairly sure others do not know about you (hidden area).

4. Make a list of _five_ things you would like to know about yourself that you suspect others may know but you do not (blind area).

5. For items 2, 3, and 4 above, identify specific communicative ways in which you can either learn more about yourself or self-disclose information to others.

Discussion: Discussion should surround why certain individuals know more about you than others; why you disclose to certain individuals as opposed to others; and conclusions you can draw about communicative improvements you would like to make. Are your areas of communicative concern shared with other class members? If you draw different Johari Windows for your various relationships, can you see a recurrent pattern in the way each quadrant relates to the other quadrants? To what degree does self-awareness and sharing information about the self enhance or detract from quality interpersonal relationships?

SELF-DISCLOSURE QUESTIONNAIRE

Goal: The purpose of this exercise is for you to identify <u>who</u> you self-disclose to and <u>what</u> you self-disclose about.

Instructions: At the end of this questionnaire is an Answer Sheet comprised of columns with the headings "Mother," "Father," "Male Friend," "Female Friend," and "Spouse." You are to read each item on the questionnaire and then indicate on the Answer Sheet the extent that you have talked about that item to each person; that is, the extent to which you have made yourself known to that person. Use the rating scale that you see on the Answer Sheet to describe the extent that you have talked about each item.

Attitudes and Opinions

1. What I think and feel about religion; my personal religious views.
2. My personal opinions and feelings about other religious groups than my own; e.g., Protestants, Catholics, Jews, atheists.
3. My views on communism.
4. My views on the present government--the president, government policies, etc.
5. My views on the question of racial integration in schools, transportation, etc.
6. My personal views on drinking.
7. My personal views on sexual morality--how I feel that I and others ought to behave in sexual matters.
8. My personal standards of beauty and attractiveness in women--what I consider to be attractive in a woman.
9. The things that I regard as desirable for a man to be--what I look for in a man.
10. My feelings about how parents ought to deal with children.

Tastes and Interests

1. My favorite foods, the ways I like food prepared, and my food dislikes.
2. My favorite beverages, and the ones I don't like.
3. My likes and dislikes in music.
4. My favorite reading matter.
5. The kinds of movies that I like to see best; the TV shows that are my favorites.
6. My tastes in clothing.
7. The style of house, and the kinds of furnishings that I like best.
8. The kind of party or social gathering that I like best, and the kind that would bore me, or that I wouldn't enjoy.
9. My favorite ways of spending spare time; e.g., hunting, reading, cards, sports events, parties, dancing, etc.
10. What I would appreciate most for a gift or present.

Work (or Studies)

1. What I find to be the worst pressures and strains in my work.
2. What I find to be the most boring and unenjoyable aspects of my work.
3. What I enjoy most, and get the most satisfaction from in my present work.
4. What I feel are my shortcomings and handicaps that prevent me from working as I'd like to, or that prevent me from getting further ahead in my work.
5. What I feel are my special strong points and qualifications for my work.
6. How I feel that my work is appreciated by others (e.g., boss, fellow workers, teacher, husband, etc.).
7. My ambitions and goals in my work.
8. My feelings about the salary or rewards that I get from my work.
9. How I feel about the choice of career that I have made--whether or not I'm satisfied with it.
10. How I really feel about the people that I work for, or work with.

Money

1. How much money I make at my work, or get as an allowance.
2. Whether or not I owe money; if so, how much.
3. Whom I owe money to at present; or whom I have borrowed from in the past.
4. Whether or not I have savings, and the amount.
5. Whether or not others owe me money; the amount, and who owes it to me.
6. Whether or not I gamble; if so, the way I gamble, and the extent of it.
7. All of my present sources of income--wages, fees, allowance, dividends, etc.
8. My total financial worth, including property, savings, bonds, insurance, etc.
9. My most pressing need for money right now, e.g., outstanding bills, some major purchase that is desired or needed.
10. How I budget my money--the proportion that goes to necessities, luxuries, etc.

Personality

1. The aspects of my personality that I dislike, worry about, that I regard as a handicap to me.
2. What feelings, if any, that I have trouble expressing or controlling.
3. The facts of my present sex life--including knowledge of how I get sexual gratification; any problems that I might have; with whom I have relations, if anybody.
4. Whether or not I feel that I am attractive to the opposite sex; my problems, if any, about getting favorable attention from the opposite sex.
5. Things in the past or present that I feel ashamed and guilty about.
6. The kinds of things that make me just furious.
7. What it takes to get me feeling depressed or blue.
8. What it takes to get me really worried, anxious, and afraid.
9. What it takes to hurt my feelings deeply.
10. The kinds of things that make me especially proud of myself, elated, full of self-esteem or self-respect.

Body

1. My feelings about the appearance of my face--things I don't like, and things that I might like about my face and head (nose, eyes, hair, teeth, etc.).
2. How I wish I looked; my ideas for overall appearance.
3. My feelings about different parts of my body--legs, hips, waist, weight, chest or bust, etc.
4. Any problems and worries that I had with my appearance in the past.
5. Whether or not I now have any health problems--e.g., trouble with sleep, digestion, female complaints, heart condition, allergies, headaches, etc.
6. Whether or not I have any long-range worries or concerns about my health, e.g., cancer, ulcers, heart trouble.
7. My past record of illness and treatment.
8. Whether or not I now make special efforts to keep fit, healthy, and attractive, e.g., exercise, diet.
9. My present physical measurements, e.g., height, weight, waist, etc.
10. My feelings about my adequacy in sexual behavior--whether or not I feel able to perform adequately in sexual relationships.

Self-Disclosure Questionnaire Answer Sheet: Use the following rating scale for each item on the "Self-Disclosure Questionnaire":

0 = Have told the other person nothing about this aspect of me.
1 = Have talked in general terms about this item. The other person has only a general idea about this aspect of me.
2 = Have talked in full and complete detail about this item to the other person. S/he knows me fully in this respect, and could describe me accurately.
X = Have lied or misrepresented myself to the other person so that s/he has a false picture of me.

Self-Disclosure

Aspect	Mother	Father	Male Friend	Female Friend	Spouse

Attitudes and Opinions

	Mother	Father	Male Friend	Female Friend	Spouse
1.	___	___	___	___	___
2.	___	___	___	___	___
3.	___	___	___	___	___
4.	___	___	___	___	___
5.	___	___	___	___	___
6.	___	___	___	___	___
7.	___	___	___	___	___
8.	___	___	___	___	___
9.	___	___	___	___	___
10.					

Self-Disclosure Aspect	Mother	Target Person Father	Male Friend	Female Friend	Spouse
Tastes and Interests					
1.	___	___	___	___	___
2.	___	___	___	___	___
3.	___	___	___	___	___
4.	___	___	___	___	___
5.	___	___	___	___	___
6.	___	___	___	___	___
7.	___	___	___	___	___
8.	___	___	___	___	___
9.	___	___	___	___	___
10.	___	___	___	___	___
Work (or Studies)					
1.	___	___	___	___	___
2.	___	___	___	___	___
3.	___	___	___	___	___
4.	___	___	___	___	___
5.	___	___	___	___	___
6.	___	___	___	___	___
7.	___	___	___	___	___
8.	___	___	___	___	___
9.	___	___	___	___	___
10.	___	___	___	___	___
Money					
1.	___	___	___	___	___
2.	___	___	___	___	___
3.	___	___	___	___	___
4.	___	___	___	___	___
5.	___	___	___	___	___
6.	___	___	___	___	___
7.	___	___	___	___	___
8.	___	___	___	___	___
9.	___	___	___	___	___
10.	___	___	___	___	___

Self-Disclosure Aspect	Mother	Target Person Father	Male Friend	Female Friend	Spouse

Personality

1. _____ _____ _____ _____ _____
2. _____ _____ _____ _____ _____
3. _____ _____ _____ _____ _____
4. _____ _____ _____ _____ _____
5. _____ _____ _____ _____ _____
6. _____ _____ _____ _____ _____
7. _____ _____ _____ _____ _____
8. _____ _____ _____ _____ _____
9. _____ _____ _____ _____ _____
10. _____ _____ _____ _____ _____

Body

1. _____ _____ _____ _____ _____
2. _____ _____ _____ _____ _____
3. _____ _____ _____ _____ _____
4. _____ _____ _____ _____ _____
5. _____ _____ _____ _____ _____
6. _____ _____ _____ _____ _____
7. _____ _____ _____ _____ _____
8. _____ _____ _____ _____ _____
9. _____ _____ _____ _____ _____
10. _____ _____ _____ _____ _____

Self-Disclosure Questionnaire Scoring Sheet

Instructions: On the Answer Sheet compute the sums for each target person in each self-disclosure aspect and copy each sum on the Scoring Sheet.

Self-Disclosure Aspect	Mother	Target Person Father	Male Friend	Female Friend	Spouse	Total
Attitudes and Opinions	_____	_____	_____	_____	_____	_____
Tastes and Interests	_____	_____	_____	_____	_____	_____
Work (or Studies)	_____	_____	_____	_____	_____	_____
Money	_____	_____	_____	_____	_____	_____
Person-ality	_____	_____	_____	_____	_____	_____
Body	_____	_____	_____	_____	_____	_____
Total	_____	_____	_____	_____	_____	_____

Put these scores on the accompanying profile sheet

Self-Disclosure Questionnaire Profile Sheet

Instructions: Draw profiles for each of your "target" persons on the chart below. You may wish to use different colored pencils. Locate your five scores for Mother, for example, and connect these with straight lines. Do the same for each of the other persons. On the scale representing your total self-disclosure scores, write the names of the target persons at their appropriate level.

Interpretation Suggestions: Studying the chart below, (1) look for similarity/dissimilarity of profiles between target persons; (2) look for high and low disclosure aspects across target persons.

```
20 _____          _____ 120
                                                      _____ 110
    _____         _____ 90
    _____         _____ 80
    _____         _____ 70
    _____         _____ 60
15  _____         _____ 50
    _____         _____ 40
    _____         _____ 30
    _____         _____ 20
    _____         _____ 10
10  _____         _____ 0

    _____
    _____      Total Self-
                                                  Disclosure
    _____      Score
5   _____
    _____
    _____
    _____
    _____
    _____

0
    Atti-   Tastes  Work  Money  Person-  Body
    tudes                       ality
```

Source: Sidney M. Jourard. *Self-Disclosure: An Experimental Analysis of the Transparent Self.* Huntington, NY: Robert E. Krieger, 1979, pp. 189-191.

SELF-DISCLOSURE EXERCISE

Goal: The purpose of this exercise is for you to identify what constitutes small talk, mild self-disclosure, and risky self-disclosing topics.

Instructions: Pair up with one other person from class. During the time allotted for this experience, you are to ask questions from this list. The questions vary in their degree of intimacy, and you may want to begin with less intimate ones. Take turns initiating the questions. Follow these rules: (a) your communication with your partner will be held in confidence; (b) you must be willing to answer any questions that you ask your partner; (c) you may decline to answer any question initiated by your partner, but if you do, you cannot later ask this same question of your partner.

1. How important is religion in your life?
2. What is the source of your financial income?
3. What is your favorite hobby or leisure interest?
4. What do you feel most ashamed of in your past?
5. What is your grade-point average at present?
6. Have you ever cheated on an examination?
7. Have you deliberately lied about a serious matter to either parent?
8. What is the most serious lie you have ever told?
9. How do you feel about couples living together without being married?
10. Do you practice masturbation?
11. Have you been arrested or fined for violating any law?
12. Have you any health problems? What are they?
13. Have you ever had a mystical experience?
14. What do you regard as your chief personality fault?
15. What turns you on the most?
16. How do you feel about interracial dating or marriage?
17. Do you consider yourself a political liberal or conservative?
18. What turns you off the fastest?
19. What features of your appearance do you consider most attractive to members of the opposite sex?
20. What do you regard as your least attractive features?
21. How important is money to you?
22. Are you or your parents divorced? Have you ever considered divorce?
23. What person would you most like to take a trip with right now?
24. How do you feel about swearing?
25. Have you ever been drunk?
26. Do you smoke marijuana or use drugs?
27. Do you enjoy manipulating or directing people?
28. Are females equal, inferior, or superior to males?
29. How often have you needed to see a doctor in the past year?
30. Have you ever been tempted to kill yourself?
31. Have you ever been tempted to kill someone else?
32. Would you participate in a public demonstration?
33. What emotions do you find most difficult to control?
34. Is there a particular person you wish would be attracted to you? Who?
35. What foods do you most dislike?

36. What are you most reluctant to discuss now?
37. To what person are you responding the most and how?
38. What is your IQ?
39. Is there any feature of your personality that you are proud of? What is it?
40. What was your worst failure, your biggest disappointment to yourself or family?
41. What is your favorite TV program?
42. What is the subject of the most serious quarrels you have had with your parents?
43. What is the subject of your most frequent daydreams?
44. How are you feeling about me?
45. What are your career goals?
46. With what do you feel the greatest need for help?
47. How do you feel about crying in the presence of others?
48. Have you ever engaged in homosexual activities?
49. If you could be anyone besides yourself, what or who would you be?
50. What quality in others do you dislike the most?

Discussion: This exercise should provide you with a list of topics that you are willing to discuss and a list of topics that you are reluctant to discuss. Those that you are reluctant to discuss constitute significant instances of self-disclosure to you. Thus, discussion should center on whether there is any pattern to the topics you are willing or unwilling to disclose about--i.e., can you talk about your fears but not your sexual practices? Are you unwilling to set yourself up to be criticized by others? Are you afraid to expose your weaknesses? Are there any taboo topics on this list? Are there any common themes among all class members' ability to talk about or not talk about certain topics? Are any of these themes culturally-bound?

TARGETS FOR SELF-DISCLOSURE

Goal: The purpose of this exercise is to identify <u>who</u> you prefer to self-disclose to about <u>what</u>.

Instructions: For each situation and topic below, identify two persons who you would self-disclose to under the conditions described. Be prepared to explain why you would target these individuals for self-disclosure.

1. <u>Situation 1</u>: You are angry at the world today. Who would you contact to unload your feelings?

   a. _____

   b. _____

2. <u>Situation 2</u>: You need someone who watch your pets for a week while you are on vacation. Who would you ask?

   a. _____

   b. _____

3. <u>Situation 3</u>: You just found out that your intimate partner is having an affair. Who would you call?

   a. _____

   b. _____

4. <u>Situation 4</u>: You have just been offered the job of a lifetime and are overjoyed. Who would you tell?

   a. _____

   b. _____

5. <u>Situation 5</u>: Your mother is in the hospital and you need to fly home to see her right away. From whom would you borrow money?

   a. _____

   b. _____

Discussion: Was it difficult selecting people for these situations? Does the situation change the depth and breadth of self-disclosure? What did you learn about these relationships and the roles they play in your life? What kind of relationship do you have with each of the persons you listed that makes self-disclosure easier for you?

LYING AND HONESTY

Goal: The purpose of this exercise is to identify when, if at all, it is acceptable to lie (or not tell the absolute truth).

Instructions:

1. Make a list of <u>five</u> lies that you have told in your recent memory. For each lie, identify <u>what</u> the lie was about, <u>who</u> was lied to, and the <u>effects</u> of the lie.

<u>Content of Lie</u>	<u>Who Was Lied To</u>	<u>Effects of Lie</u>
a. _____		
b. _____		
c. _____		
d. _____		
e. _____		

2. Pair up with another member of the class and discuss your lies. You should evaluate your own and your partners' lies and determine whether the effects of being honest would have been worse than the effects of having told the lie.

3. Generate a list of situations or conditions where lying is acceptable; then generate a list that identifies when lying is not acceptable (or when honestly would be the best policy). Prepare to discuss your list with the whole class.

Discussion: Your discussion should center on whether lying is always bad or honestly is always good. When you lie to someone you care about, what are you really telling that person? How do you feel when you lie, even if you feel it is justified? How do you feel if you find out that someone else has lied to you? Can you be completely honest with others? Do you want to be completely honest with others?

DIFFERENT APPROACHES
TO CONFLICT

Win/Lose Approach

1. Clear we/they distinctions between people rather than a we-vs-they problem orientation.

2. Energies directed toward the other party in an atmosphere of defeat or victory.

3. Seeing the issue only from your own point of view, rather than defining the problem in terms of mutual needs.

4. Emphasis on the process of attaining a solution rather than on the definition of goals, values, or motives to be attained within the solution.

5. Conflicts are personalized.

6. People are conflict-oriented, emphasizing the disagreement, rather than relationship-oriented, emphasizing the long term effects of their differences on how they are resolved.

7. Defensive communication climate: evaluative, controlling, strategic communication given in superior, nonempathetic, and certain ways.

Win/Win Approach

1. Focusing on common goals of all people involved rather than different goals and/or means of accomplishing goals.

2. Focusing on the common problems, not on the participants, i.e., defeat of the problem, not of each other.

3. All participants' expressions of their needs and their interpretations of the situation.

4. Development of a sense of we-ness rather than a polarized us-vs-they.

5. Equal participation by all group members.

6. Use of consensus methods of decision-making rather than avoiding conflict by voting, trading, or compromising.

7. Sharing all available information rather than guarding information strategically.

8. Predictable responses so that trust begins to be established.

9. Supportive communication behaviors: description, spontaneity, empathy, equality, and provisionalism.

THOMAS-KILMANN CONFLICT MODE
INSTRUMENT

Goal: The purpose of this instrument is for you to identify and rank order the styles you most often use in conflict situations.

Instructions: Consider the situations in which you find your wishes differing from those of another person. How do you usually respond to such situations? On the following pages are several pairs of statements describing possible behavioral responses. For each pair, please circle the "A" or "B" statement which is most characteristic of your own behavior. In many cases, neither the "A" nor the "B" statement may be very typical of your behavior; but please select the response which you would be more likely to use.

1.   A.   There are times when I let others take responsibility for solving the problem.
      B.   Rather than negotiate the things on which we disagree, I try to stress those things upon which we both agree.

2.   A.   I try to find a compromise solution.
      B.   I attempt to deal with all of his/her and my concerns.

3.   A.   I am usually firm in pursuing my goals.
      B.   I might try to soothe the other's feelings and preserve our relationship.

4.   A.   I try to find a compromise solution.
      B.   I sometimes sacrifice my own wishes for the wishes of the other person.

5.   A.   I consistently seek the other's help in working out a solution.
      B.   I try to do what is necessary to avoid useless tension.

6.   A.   I try to avoid creating unpleasantness for myself.
      B.   I try to win my position.

7.   A.   I try to postpone the issue until I have had some time to think it over.
      B.   I give up some points in exchange for others.

8.   A.   I am usually firm in pursuing my goals.
      B.   I attempt to get all concerns and issues immediately out in the open.

9.   A.   I feel that differences are not always worth worrying about.
      B.   I make some effort to get my way.

10.   A.   I am firm in pursuing my goals.
      B.   I try to find a compromise solution.

11. A. I attempt to get all concerns and issues immediately out in the open.
    B. I might try to soothe the other's feelings and preserve our relationship.

12. A. I sometimes avoid taking positions which would create controversy.
    B. I will let others have some of their positions if they let me have some of mine.

13. A. I propose a middle ground.
    B. I press to get my points made.

14. A. I tell him/her my ideas and ask him/her for his/hers.
    B. I try to show him/her the logic and benefits of my position.

15. A. I might try to soothe the other's feelings and preserve our relationship.
    B. I try to do what is necessary to avoid tensions.

16. A. I try not to hurt the other's feelings.
    B. I try to convince the other person of the merits of my position.

17. A. I am usually firm in pursuing my goals.
    B. I try to do what is necessary to avoid useless tensions.

18. A. If it makes the other person happy, I might let him/her maintain her/his views.
    B. I will let him/her have some of his/her positions if s/he lets me have some of mine.

19. A. I attempt to get all concerns and issues immediately out in the open.
    B. I try to postpone the issue until I have had some time to think it over.

20. A. I attempt to immediately work through our differences.
    B. I try to find a fair combination of gains and losses for both of us.

21. A. In approaching negotiations, I try to be considerate of the other person's wishes.
    B. I always lean toward a direct discussion of the problem.

22. A. I try to find a position that is intermediate between hers/his and mine.
    B. I assert my wishes.

23. A. I am very often concerned with satisfying all our wishes.
    B. There are times when I let others take responsibility for solving the problem.

Scoring the Thomas-Kilmann Conflict Mode Instrument

Instructions: Circle the letter below which you circled on each item of the questionnaire.

	Compet- ing (forcing)	Collaborat- ing (problem- solving)	Compromis- ing (sharing)	Avoid- ing (with- drawal)	Accommo- dating (smooth- ing)
1.				A	B
2.		B	A		
3.	A				B
4.			A		B
5.		A		B	
6.	B			A	
7.			B	A	
8.	A	B			
9.	B			A	
10.	A		B		
11.		A			B
12.			B	A	
13.	B		A		
14.	B	A			
15.				B	A
16.	B				A
17.	A			B	
18.			B		A
19.		A		B	
20.		A	B		
21.		B			A
22.	B		A		
23.		A		B	
24.			B		A
25.	A				B
26.		B	A		
27.				A	B
28.	A	B			
29.			A	B	
30.		B			A

Total the number of items circled in each column:

Competing	Collaborating	Compromising	Avoiding	Accommodating

24.   A.   If the other's position seems very important to him/her, I would try to meet his/her wishes.
      B.   I try to get him/her to settle for a compromise.

25.   A.   I try to show her/him the logic and benefits of my position.
      B.   In approaching negotiations, I try to be considerate of the other person's wishes.

26.   A.   I propose a middle ground.
      B.   I am nearly always concerned with satisfying all our wishes.

27.   A.   I sometimes avoid taking positions that would create controversy.
      B.   If it makes the other person happy, I might let her/him maintain his/her views.

28.   A.   I am usually firm in pursuing my goals.
      B.   I usually seek the other's help in working out a solution.

29.   A.   I propose a middle ground.
      B.   I feel that differences are not always worth worrying about.

30.   A.   I try not to hurt the other's feelings.
      B.   I always share the problem with the other person so that we can work it out.

Interpreting Your Scores on the Thomas-Kilmann Conflict Mode Instrument

The Five Conflict Handling Modes: The Thomas-Kilman Conflict Mode Instrument is designed to assess an individual's behavior in conflict situations. "Conflict Situations" are situations in which the concerns of two people appear to be incompatible. In such situations, we can describe a person's behavior along two basic dimensions: (1) assertiveness, the extent to which the individual attempts to satisfy his/her own concerns, and (2) cooperativeness, the extent to which the individual attempts to satisfy the other's concern. These two basic dimensions of behavior can be used to define five specific methods of dealing with conflicts. These five "conflict-handling modes" are shown below.

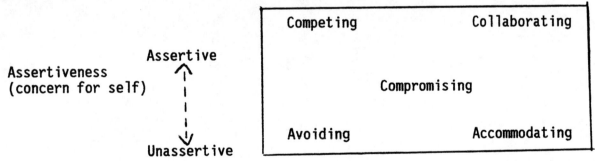

Source: Kenneth W. Thomas, and Ralph H. Kilmann. Thomas-Kilmann Conflict MODE Instrument. Tuxedo, NY: Xicon, 1974.

PUTNAM/WILSON CONFLICT BEHAVIOR SCALE

Goal: To identify the typical or recurrent ways in which you communicate when involved in a conflict with another person.

Instructions: Think of a conflict you have encountered in task situations with your peers. Then indicate below how frequently you engage in each of the described behaviors. Respond to the items with a _particular_ conflict in mind. For each item select the number that represents the behavior you are _most likely_ to exhibit. There are no right or wrong answers. Please respond to all items on the scale. The alternative are:

7 = Always	3 = Seldom	
6 = Very Often	2 = Very Seldom	
5 = Often	4 = Sometimes	1 = Never

Conflict Behaviors

1. I blend my new ideas with others to create new solutions to conflict.
   Never 1 2 3 4 5 6 7 Always

2. I shy away from topics which are sources of disputes.
   Never 1 2 3 4 5 6 7 Always

3. I insist my position be accepted during a conflict.
   Never 1 2 3 4 5 6 7 Always

4. I try to find solutions which combine a variety of viewpoints.
   Never 1 2 3 4 5 6 7 Always

5. I steer clear of disagreeable situations.
   Never 1 2 3 4 5 6 7 Always

6. I give in a little on my ideas when others also give in.
   Never 1 2 3 4 5 6 7 Always

7. I look for middle-of-the-road solutions.
   Never 1 2 3 4 5 6 7 Always

8. I avoid a person I suspect of wanting to discuss a disagreement.
   Never 1 2 3 4 5 6 7 Always

9. I minimize the significance of a conflict.
   Never 1 2 3 4 5 6 7 Always

10. I build an integrated solution from the issues raised in a dispute.
    Never 1 2 3 4 5 6 7 Always

11. I stress my point by hitting my fist on the table.
    Never 1 2 3 4 5 6 7 Always

12. I will go 50-50 to reach a settlement.
    Never 1 2 3 4 5 6 7 Always

13. I raise my voice when trying to get others to accept my position.
   Never   1 2 3 4 5 6 7   Always

14. I look for creative solutions to conflicts.
   Never   1 2 3 4 5 6 7   Always

15. I keep quiet about my views in order to avoid disagreements.
   Never   1 2 3 4 5 6 7   Always

16. I'm willing to give in a little if the other person will meet me halfway.
   Never   1 2 3 4 5 6 7   Always

17. I downplay the importance of a disagreement.
   Never   1 2 3 4 5 6 7   Always

18. I reduce disagreements by making them seem insignificant.
   Never   1 2 3 4 5 6 7   Always

19. I will meet the opposition midway to reach a settlement.
   Never   1 2 3 4 5 6 7   Always

20. I assert my opinion forcefully.
   Never   1 2 3 4 5 6 7   Always

21. I dominate arguments until others accept my position.
   Never   1 2 3 4 5 6 7   Always

22. I encourage working together to create solutions to disagreements.
   Never   1 2 3 4 5 6 7   Always

23. I try to use everyone's ideas to generate solutions to problems.
   Never   1 2 3 4 5 6 7   Always

24. I make trade-offs to reach solutions.
   Never   1 2 3 4 5 6 7   Always

25. I argue insistently for my stance.
   Never   1 2 3 4 5 6 7   Always

26. I withdraw when someone confronts me about a controversial issue.
   Never   1 2 3 4 5 6 7   Always

27. I sidestep disagreements when they arise.
   Never   1 2 3 4 5 6 7   Always

28. I try to smooth over disagreements by making them appear unimportant.
   Never   1 2 3 4 5 6 7   Always

29. I insist my position be accepted during a conflict.
   Never   1 2 3 4 5 6 7   Always

30. I take a tough stand refusing to retreat.
   Never   1 2 3 4 5 6 7   Always

31. I settle differences by meeting the other person halfway.
     Never 1 2 3 4 5 6 7 Always

32. I am steadfast in my views.
     Never 1 2 3 4 5 6 7 Always

33. I make our differences seem less serious.
     Never 1 2 3 4 5 6 7 Always

34. I hold my tongue rather than argue.
     Never 1 2 3 4 5 6 7 Always

35. I ease conflict by claiming our differences are trivial.
     Never 1 2 3 4 5 6 7 Always

After you have completed your own conflict behavior scale, fill out the same scale to indicate your perception of your conflict partner's behavior.

Scoring Instructions::

1. Add your scores for questionnaire items numbered 2, 5, 8, 15, 17, 18, 26, 27, 28, 33, 34, 35. Take the total, divide by 12 and you have your average score on this item dimension of nonconfrontation. A high numerical score (7) means you use the style more often.

2. Add your scores for items numbered 1, 4, 6, 10, 12, 14, 16, 19, 22, 23, 24. Take the total and divide by 11. This results in your average score on solution-orientation. A high score means you use this style more often.

3. Add your scores for items numbered 3, 7, 9, 11, 13, 20, 21, 25, 29, 30, 31, 32. Divide the total by 12, and the answer is your average score on control, with a high number meaning you use it more often.

4. Then compare your average scores on all three dimensions to see which style you use most and least often. Remember, a high numerical score signifies you use the style more often.

Discussion: Do your most preferred styles lead to the results and satisfaction you desire? In other words, are your conflicts typically managed productively? Why or why not? Do you ever employ your least preferred styles? Why or why not? How can you communicatively learn to rely less on your most preferred styles and more on your least preferred styles?

Source: Linda L. Putnam, and C. Wilson. "Communicative Strategies in Organizational Conflict: Reliability and Validity of a Measurement Scale," in Communication Yearbook, Volume 6, ed. Michael Burgoon. Newbury Park, CA: Sage, 1982: 629-652.

DEALING WITH ANGER AND HOSTILITY
IN OTHERS

1. Remember that anger comes from fear. What are the parties fearful of? How does the fear trigger their anger?

2. Acknowledge your own defensiveness in an honest and appropriate way when people are angry.

3. Request more negative information when people are angry instead of shutting them off. Say "I need to know more about that," or "I didn't know you thought that. Tell me how you came to that conclusion."

4. Open channels of communication. Use the phone, face-to-face contact, more notes, more meetings.

5. Ask for the other person's <u>interests</u> in solving the problem. Try to ignore statements of <u>position</u>. Work toward common goals.

6. Restate and actively listen to the other person's interests. Help him or her express the anger directly and appropriately.

7. Ask if the other person will listen to you too.

8. Speak of your own interests, your goals, and your perception of your shared concerns.

9. Avoid defensive-provoking statements such as heavy control talk and evaluation.

10. Never say "You shouldn't be angry." Feelings are facts.

11. State your feelings accurately, but in moderation. Don't drop the bomb unless you want to start a war. Catharsis should be reserved for intimates.

12. Continuously state that you expect that you will be able to work this out together.

13. Ask for suggestions for solving the problem together. Initiate collaborative suggestions yourself.

14. Use productive negotiation techniques when the person calms down. Until then, acknowledge feelings more than ideas.

15. End with "I want to keep this from happening again. What can be done to learn from today?"

Source: Joyce Hocker, and William W. Wilmot. <u>Interpersonal Communication</u> (Instructor's Manual), 3rd ed. Dubuque, Iowa: William C. Brown, 1991, p. 63.

CONFLICT SCENARIOS

Goal: The purpose of this exercise is to distinguish between win/win and win/lose approaches to conflict.

Instructions: Form groups of 4-6 persons.   You will be assigned one of the following six scenarios.   Read it carefully.   Then construct both a win/win solution and a win/lose solution for that scenario.   Be prepared to role play each solution in front of the class.

1.   Johnny has given Michelle permission to use his stereo, but Michelle is not as careful with the equipment as is Johnny. Johnny thinks Michelle is disrespectful of his possessions, and Michelle thinks Johnny is overprotective of his stereo.   Since they are roommates, and Michelle will probably use Johnny's stereo anyway, Johnny approaches Michelle and decides that it is time to settle this conflict.

2.   Patty has had a crush on Ted for a long time. Mary is a close friend of Patty's.   Ted has been persistently chasing Mary, and Mary has finally agreed to go out with Ted. Patty finds out and confronts Mary.

3.   Jamie and Kevin are roommates.   Jamie has all the bills in her name. Kevin pays his share directly to Jamie. Kevin has unwittingly been the victim of a mix-up at the bank and wrote Jamie a bad check.   Jamie deposited the check, and in turn, has written a number of bad checks. Jamie confronts Kevin, certain that Kevin knows what happened. Kevin does not, but even if he did, he feels Jamie approached him poorly.

4.   Marcie and Frank have been married for nearly two years.   Both of them have careers and enjoy their work. Frank wants children; Marcie, however, is nervous around small children, especially babies. Frank wants to start a family, but Marcie is hesitant. When Frank tells Marcie his feelings, Marcie initiates conversation about this issue.

5.   Tom and Jan have dated for five years.   They met in high school and attended the same college. Jan enjoys the relationship, but isn't really serious about Tom. Tom, however, assumes they will eventually be married. Jan has just decided to attend medical school at Harvard, and knows that Tom plans to stay in California and work. She shares her plans with Tom.

Discussion: Which kind of conflict resolution is easiest to envision? If you were emotionally involved in this conflict, could you generate a win/win solution? How likely would it be for each party to feel like a victim? Is trust and goodwill a prerequisite for a win/win solution?

CONSTRUCTIVELY MANAGING CONFLICTS

Goal: To develop skills in managing relationship conflicts effectively.

Instructions: Think of a recent conflict in your life which was not managed well, or one that resulted in an escalation rather than a resolution to tension. Write a brief summary of this conflict, including who was involved, what kinds of messages and behaviors were used by each participant, the outcome of the conflict, and the effects of this conflict on your relationship. Form groups of 4 persons. All members should briefly summarize their conflicts for the group. The group should then use the following four negotiation techniques to collect information, gain understanding, and discover possible ways to resolve the conflict. These enable constructive negotiation in conflict.

Four Principles of Conflict Negotiation:

Identify the Problem: What specific problem triggered the conflict? Try to identify <u>one</u> primary issue (point of contention), but realize that the conflict may incorporate more than one issue. Typically your conflict is over a <u>content</u> issue (a particular topic, behavior, or thing), or it may be over a <u>relational</u> issue (important concepts defining the relationship like power, affection, security, appreciation, time, attention, independence, etc.). In general, if this conflict is recurrent, then the issue is relational in nature. The point here is that in order to manage your conflict productively, you must identify the problem(s) accounting for the conflict. To clarify your conflict, make sure that you <u>separate</u> the people from the problem, i.e., the problem exists regardless of who the people are in the conflict.

Identify Interest in Resolving the Problem: You need to gauge the level of interest or commitment each party has in resolving or managing the conflict. So, instead of simply stating and defending your position or demands (your interests), focus on <u>shared</u> interests: "What do we want to come out of this conflict?" "What do we gain or lose by continuing this conflict?" "What can we do to ease the tensions?" If you both are committed to working on a resolution, then you are focusing on areas of agreement, not disagreement, and this is the first step in productive conflict management. If you or the other party is not committed to conflict resolution, then there is little point in expending energy. If no joint commitment exists, then it is likely that the issue you identify is <u>not</u> the real conflict anyway; rather, it is likely to be a relational issue, probably about the nature of commitment to the relationship.

Create Options for Conflict Resolution: Brainstorm and generate as many possible solutions to the problem(s) you identify. Good decisions--and ones that parties will commit to--spring from having multiple options.

Generate Objective Criteria: The decision you both agree upon needs to be based on some objective standard, such as what is fair and equitable for both parties. So, in addition to making a decision, make sure that you identify a rationale or reasonable justification for that decision.

Discussion: How difficult is it to clarify conflict issues, especially relationship issues? Can you separate people from the problem? What are the benefits of giving reasons for decisions? Why do we work against not with others? How can you request a conflict negotiation session with another?

112

RELATIONAL COMMUNICATION

Attitudes toward Intimate Communication

Communication Patterns in Relationships

Improving Relational Communication

THE IDEAL RELATIONSHIP

Goal: The purpose of this exercise is to identify assumptions we have about enduring intimate relationships and the role of communication in that relationship.

Instructions: Make a list of the qualities that you would like in an intimate relationship if you could have a perfect relationship. Then interview three other people and have them describe their own concept of the ideal relationship. Synthesize this information by answering the following questions, and be prepared to discuss your results in class.

1.   What common themes are expressed about the ideal _man_? _____
     _____
     _____
     _____
     _____

2.   What common themes are expressed about the ideal _woman_? _____
     _____
     _____
     _____
     _____

3.   What common themes surround the nature of the _relationship_? _____
     _____
     _____
     _____
     _____

4.   What kinds of _communication_ patterns exist in the ideal relationship? _____
     _____
     _____
     _____
     _____

Discussion: Discussion should surround what assumptions are being made about relationships, and whether those assumptions set up realistic or unrealistic expectations about intimate relationships. In addition, do images about a relationship differ depending upon cultural differences? Is it possible to describe a relationship without referring to communication skills?

MARITAL ROLES

Goal: The purpose of this exercise is for you to identify and clarify your expectations for a spouse.

Instructions: For the following items, respond by indicating what you believe is right as a matter of principle using the scoring system below: Strongly Agree = 5, Agree = 4, Undecided = 3, Disagree = 2, Strongly Disagree = 1. Complete the statements individually; then, in groups of 4-6, compare and discuss your respective responses.

_____ 1. The wife should have primary responsibility for children.
_____ 2. The husband should help with household chores.
_____ 3. The wife should have a career.
_____ 4. The wife should have primary responsibility for the children.
_____ 5. If a husband has an extramarital affair, the wife should be able to also.
_____ 6. A husband should have a life independent of his wife.
_____ 7. The husband should be the primary breadwinner in the family.
_____ 8. Husbands are not responsible enough around the house.
_____ 9. If a wife wants children, the husband should submit to her wishes.
_____ 10. Wives should trust their husbands more.
_____ 11. The wife should take the husband's name upon marriage.
_____ 12. The wife should take care of the finances of the household.
_____ 13. Wives should be more independent than they are.
_____ 14. Wives should be disciplined by their husbands.
_____ 15. The husband should make the decision about where the couple will live.
_____ 16. The husband's career should take precedence over the wife's career.
_____ 17. Marriage should take precedence over career for wives.
_____ 18. What wives want should take precedence over what husbands want in most circumstances.
_____ 19. Husbands should make most of the decisions in the family.
_____ 20. The wife should take primary responsibility for making sure her husband is happy in the marriage.

Discussion: Discussion should surround to what degree women and men differ in their views about marital roles. In addition, are your expectations reasonable and compatible with your knowledge of marriage in our contemporary society? To what degree do cultural differences play a role in influencing your attitudes about wives' and husbands' roles in marriage?

THE MARRIAGE QUIZ

Goal: To identify myths and facts about marriage, and to compare your attitudes toward marriage to research findings on marriage.

Instructions: Complete the marriage quiz by responding "True" or "False" to the twenty statements provided below. Prepare an explanation for your response.

_____ 1. A husband's marital satisfaction is usually lower if his wife is employed fulltime than if she is a fulltime homemaker.

_____ 2. Today, most young, single people will eventually get married.

_____ 3. Having a child improves marital satisfaction for both spouses.

_____ 4. The best predictor of overall marital satisfaction is the quality of a couple's sex life.

_____ 5. The divorce rate in America increased from 1960 to 1980.

_____ 6. A greater percentage of wives are working now than in 1970.

_____ 7. Marital satisfaction for a wife is usually lower if she is employed fulltime than if she is a fulltime homemaker.

_____ 8. My spouse should instinctively know what I want and need to be happy.

_____ 9. In a marriage in which the wife is employed fulltime, the husband usually assumes an equal share of the housekeeping duties.

_____ 10. For most couples, marital satisfaction gradually increases from the first year of marriage through the childbearing years, the teen years, the empty nest period, and retirement.

_____ 11. My spouse should love me no matter how I behave.

_____ 12. One of the most frequent marital problems is poor communication.

_____ 13. Husbands usually make more life style adjustments than wives.

_____ 14. Couples who cohabitated before marriage usually report greater marital satisfaction than couples who did not.

_____ 15. I can change my spouse by pointing out his/her inadequacies.

_____ 16. Couples who marry when they are under the age of 18 have a greater chance of divorcing than those who marry when they are older.

_____ 17. Either my spouse loves me or does not love me; nothing I do will affect her/his feelings about me.

_____ 18. The more a spouse self-discloses both positive and negative information to his/her partner, the greater the marital satisfaction.

_____ 19. I must feel better about my partner before I can change my behavior toward her/him.

_____ 20. Maintaining romantic love is the key to marital happiness over the life span for most couples.

Discussion: The marriage quiz is based on what research has found to be true of most relationships; your responses may well differ from these findings. Keep in mind that your tendency may be to say "this is true of other people, not me." Also realize that relationships require attention: no one magical person will make the rest of your life happy. Given this, is our contemporary notion of marriage different from traditional assumptions about marriage? Can you identify similarities and differences? How accurate or inaccurate are your perceptions about marriage? To what degree is communication important in a happy marriage?

Source: Jeffrey H. Larson. "The Marriage Quiz." Family Relations, 37 (1988): 3-11. Answers to the Marriage Quiz can be found in the appendix at the end of the workbook.

LOVE STYLES PROFILE

Goal: To identify your assumptions and preferences about love, and to identify your own styles of love.

Instructions: Place the number that best represents your attitude in the space next to each statement. Use the following scale:

> 1 = strongly agree
> 2 = agree
> 3 = neutral
> 4 = disagree
> 5 = strongly disagree

_____ 1. My lover and I were attracted to each other immediately after we first met.

_____ 2. My lover and I have the right physical "chemistry" between us.

_____ 3. Our lovemaking is very intense and satisfying.

_____ 4. I feel that my lover and I were meant for each other.

_____ 5. My lover and I became emotionally involved rather quickly.

_____ 6. My lover and I really understand each other.

_____ 7. My lover fits my ideal standards of physical beauty or handsomeness.

_____ 8. I try to keep my lover a little uncertain about my commitment to her/him.

_____ 9. I believe that what my lover doesn't know about me won't hurt him/her.

_____ 10. I have sometimes had to keep my lover from finding out about other lovers.

_____ 11. I could get over my love affair with my lover pretty easily and quickly.

_____ 12. My lover would get upset if s/he knew of some of the things I've done with other people.

_____ 13. When my lover gets too dependent on me, I want to back off a little.

_____ 14. I enjoy playing the "game of love" with my lover and a number of other partners.

_____ 15. It is hard for me to say exactly when our friendship turned into love.

_____ 16. To be genuine, our love first required caring for a while.

_____ 17. I expect to always be friends with my lover.

_____ 18. Our love is the best kind because it grew out of a long friendship.

_____ 19. Our friendship merged gradually into love over time.

_____ 20. Our love is really a deep friendship, not a mysterious, mystical emotion.

_____ 21. Our love relationship is the most satisfying because it developed from a good friendship.

_____ 22. I considered what my lover was going to become in life before I committed myself to her/him.

_____ 23. I tried to plan my life carefully before choosing a lover.

_____ 24. In choosing my lover, I believed it was best to love someone with a similar background.

_____ 25. A main consideration in choosing my lover was how s/he would reflect on my family.

_____ 26. An important factor in choosing my lover was whether or not s/he would be a good parent.

_____ 27. One consideration in choosing my lover was how s/he would reflect on my career.

_____ 28. Before getting very involved with my lover, I tried to figure out how compatible his/her hereditary background would be with mine in case we ever had children.

_____ 29. When things aren't right with my lover and me, my stomach gets upset.

_____ 30. If my lover and I break up, I would get so depressed that I would even think of suicide.

_____ 31. Sometimes I get so excited about being in love with my lover that I can't sleep.

_____ 32. When my lover doesn't pay attention to me, I feel sick all over.

_____ 33. Since I've been in love with my lover, I've had trouble concentrating on anything else.

_____ 34. I cannot relax if I suspect that my lover is with someone else.

_____ 35. If my lover ignores me for a while, I sometimes do stupid things to try to get her/his attention back.

_____ 36. I try to always help my lover through difficult times.

_____ 37. I would rather suffer myself than let my lover suffer.

_____ 38. I cannot be happy unless I place my lover's happiness before my own.

_____ 39. I am usually willing to sacrifice my own wishes to let my lover achieve his/hers.

_____ 40. Whatever I own is my lover's to use as s/he chooses.

_____ 41. When my lover gets angry with me, I still love her/him fully and unconditionally.

_____ 42. I would endure all things for the sake of my lover.

Scoring: Add your ratings for statements 1 - 7. This is your score for love of beauty or passionate love. Your total for statements 8 - 14 is your score for game-playing or playful love. Your total for statements 15 - 21 is your score for friendship or companionate love. Your total for statements 22 - 28 is your score for realistic love. Your total for statements 29 - 35 is your score for obsessive love. Your total for statements 36 - 42 is your score for altruistic love. Mark your total score for each of the six types of love in the space provided on the next page. Then read the accompanying description. In general, the lower your score, the more positive your attitude is toward that type of love. A score of 7 reflects strong positive attitudes; a score close to 35 reflects strong negative attitudes toward this type of love.

____ **Passionate Love** (score on statements 1 - 7):

Passionate love is an ideal love of beauty. It is intense, immediate, and powerful. It involves physical intimacy, touching, and emotional peaks and valleys.

____ **Playful Love** (score on statements 8 - 14):

Playful love is a love of games. It involves challenging and conquering. The reward is winning the prize. The player tends to be confident and independent. The player also desires good times and may be lacking in commitment.

____ **Companionate Love** (score on statements 15 - 21):

Companionate love is love that grows naturally and peacefully. It involves affection, friendship, stability, and predictability. Partners are less likely to be preoccupied with one another, and the relationship can become too dull.

____ **Realistic Love** (score on statements 22 - 28):

Realistic love is love based on compatibility, practicality, planning, and logic. The role of feelings is minimized, and partners tend not to be able to adjust easily to changes.

____ **Obsessive Love** (score on statements 29 - 35):

Obsessive love is addictive love. The lover can be the object of dependency and manipulation. It is possessive, all-consuming, and difficult to satisfy. It is characterized by high emotional peaks and valleys, and can generate pain and jealousy.

____ **Altruistic Love** (score on statements 36 - 42):

Altruistic love is unselfish, patient, kind, generous, and reciprocal. An altruistic lover is rarely demanding, but too much concern for the other can become a relational problem as it can be stifling.

Source: C. Hendrick, and S. Hendrick. "A Relationship Specific Version of the Love Attitudes Scale," in Handbook of Replication Research in the Behavioral and Social Sciences, ed. J. W. Newliep. Journal of Social Behavior and Personality, Special Issue, 5 (1990): 239-254.

YOUR INTIMACY QUOTIENT

Goal: To identify the degree to which you are willing to express intimacy verbally and nonverbally in your relationships.

Instructions: Respond to each of the statements by using the following scale: 1 = never; 2 = seldom; 3 = often.

_____ 1. You spend time and energy cultivating and tending your friendships.

_____ 2. You maintain friendships with members of the opposite sex with whom you are not romantically involved.

_____ 3. You like to touch and be touched in affectionate ways.

_____ 4. You enjoy solitude without being lonely with your different moods and are comfortable with different moods and feelings.

_____ 5. You feel naturally high either alone or in the company of others without ever needing the help of alcohol or drugs.

_____ 6. You feel accepted, cherished, valued, and understood by your family and friends.

_____ 7. You express feelings of anger as well as feelings of tenderness, display grief as well as joy with those individuals closest to you.

_____ 8. You enjoy listening to people's life stories and philosophies and try to figure out what makes them tick.

_____ 9. You share with others your secret shames as well as your dreams, your self-doubts along with your cherished hopes.

_____ 10. You can tell what other people are feeling and empathize with them.

_____ 11. Other people seem friendly and respond generously when you make an effort to show them you care.

_____ 12. Personal intimacy for you is a way of expressing and sharing your feelings of closeness to another.

_____ **TOTAL SCORE**

Scoring Summary: Your intimacy quotient is:
LOW if you scored in the neighborhood of 12
MEDIUM if you scored in the neighborhood of 24
HIGH if you scored in the neighborhood of 36

Discussion: To check your intimacy quotient, ask a person with whom you are intimate to answer the above questions about you and then compare your respective responses. Can you identify specific verbal and nonverbal behaviors that express intimacy? To what degree does the display of intimacy affect your close relationships?

Source: Sam Keen. "Your Intimacy Quotient." Family Weekly, 22 January, 1984.

SMALL TALK

Goal: To identify your strengths and weaknesses in engaging in small talk, and to uncover topics available to you in small talk.

Instructions: Small talk is safe, superficial, social communication. Its primary functions are to maintain a sense of community with others, discover common topics, reduce uncertainty, audition for the future of a relationship with another person, and kill time. For this exercise, pair off with another class member. You will engage in small talk conversation for ten minutes. There should be no major breaks in conversation or uncomfortable periods of silence. During this conversation, make sure you include all of the following questions and statements.

1. Demographic Information:

   a. Ask at least one question about the other's name, major, occupation, career goal, birthplace, or high school attended.

   b. Offer at least one statement regarding your name, major, occupation, career goal, birthplace, or high school attended.

2. Environmental Information:

   a. Ask your partner at least one question about your immediate environment; i.e., another student in class, the classroom, the teacher, the campus, or the weather.

   b. Offer at least one statement regarding another student in class, the classroom, the teacher, the campus, or the weather.

3. Gender Topic Information:

   a. If your partner is female, ask at least one question about food, weight, clothing or attire, grooming, children, or how good or bad men are. If you are female, make at least one statement about one or more of the topics above.

   b. If your partner is male, ask at least one question about cars, sports, what happened to him last weekend, or how many women he has dated or he considers significant in his life. If you are male, make at least one statement about one or more of the topics above.

Discussion: Discussion should center on how easily you are able to maintain fluid conversation while moving from one topic to another. Which kind of information was most difficult to talk about? Which information was easiest? Was it easier for you to ask questions than make statements, or vice versa? Do you enjoy participating in small talk? Why or why not? Are the gender topics mentioned above stereotypical? Do men and women still differ in small talk topics?

"I LOVE YOU"

Goal: To identify the meanings of the phrase "I Love You."

Instructions: Complete all of the questions below. Then form groups of 4-6 persons and compare your results with them. Identify common themes, meanings, and contexts for saying "I Love You," and look for any gender differences in the use of this phrase.

1. When was the last time you said the words "I Love You" outloud? To whom or what was this addressed? Where was this stated? What were the effects or consequences of having said this? How did you feel about saying it?

   _____
   _____
   _____
   _____

2. To whom do you most frequently say "I Love You?" Identify the kind of relationship, the context in which it is most often stated, and the consequences of having said this.

   _____
   _____
   _____
   _____

3. When you tell another person "I Love You," what do you mean? Try to identify what you are really saying to the other. Does the phrase mean different things to you at different times? Try to identify specifically the meanings you attach.

   _____
   _____
   _____
   _____

4. Do you intend something different when you tell your mother and father that you love them versus when you tell your girl/boyfriend that you love her or him? What are those differences?

   _____
   _____
   _____
   _____

Discussion: Compare how frequently you say "I Love You" with how often other group members do the same. How many different meanings are there for this phrase? Are they related to emotions? power? expectations? Are there fears about telling another you love her/him? What are those fears? Are there cultural differences in the meaning and frequency of declaring love?

SEXUAL COMMUNICATION SATISFACTION INVENTORY

Goal: The degree to which intimate partners are satisfied sexually is directly related to their ability to talk freely about their sexual experiences and desires. This questionnaire is designed to identify the quality and quantity of your communication about sex to your partner.

Instructions: Indicate your level of agreement or disagreement for each of the items below by circling the number that best represents your attitude.

1. I tell my partner when I am especially sexually satisfied.
    Strongly Agree   7 6 5 4 3 2 1   Strongly Disagree

2. I am satisfied with my partner's ability to communicate her/his sexual desires to me.
    Strongly Agree   7 6 5 4 3 2 1   Strongly Disagree

3. I do not let my partner know things that I find pleasing during sex.
    Strongly Agree   1 2 3 4 5 6 7   Strongly Disagree

4. I am very satisfied with the quality of our sexual interactions.
    Strongly Agree   7 6 5 4 3 2 1   Strongly Disagree

5. I do not hesitate to let my partner know when I want to have sex with him/her.
    Strongly Agree   7 6 5 4 3 2 1   Strongly Disagree

6. I do not tell my partner whether or not I am sexually satisfied.
    Strongly Agree   1 2 3 4 5 6 7   Strongly Disagree

7. I am dissatisfied over the degree to which my partner and I discuss our sexual relationship.
    Strongly Agree   1 2 3 4 5 6 7   Strongly Disagree

8. I am not afraid to show my partner what kind of sexual behavior I find satisfying.
    Strongly Agree   7 6 5 4 3 2 1   Strongly Disagree

9. I would not hesitate to show my partner what is a sexual turn-on for me.
    Strongly Agree   7 6 5 4 3 2 1   Strongly Disagree

10. My partner does not show me when she/he is sexually satisfied.
    Strongly Agree   1 2 3 4 5 6 7   Strongly Disagree

11. I show my partner what pleases me during sex.
    Strongly Agree   7 6 5 4 3 2 1   Strongly Disagree

12. I am displeased with the manner in which my partner and I communicate with each other during sex.
    Strongly Agree   1 2 3 4 5 6 7   Strongly Disagree

13. My partner does not show me things she/he finds pleasing during sex.
    Strongly Agree   1 2 3 4 5 6 7   Strongly Disagree

14. I show my partner when I am sexually satisfied.
    Strongly Agree   7 6 5 4 3 2 1   Strongly Disagree

15. My partner does not let me know whether sex has been satisfying or not.
    Strongly Agree   1 2 3 4 5 6 7   Strongly Disagree

16. I do not show my partner when I am sexually satisfied.
    Strongly Agree   1 2 3 4 5 6 7   Strongly Disagree

17. I am satisfied concerning my ability to communicate about sexual matters
    with my partner.
    Strongly Agree   7 6 5 4 3 2 1   Strongly Disagree

18. My partner shows me by the way she/he touches me if he/she is satisfied.
    Strongly Agree   7 6 5 4 3 2 1   Strongly Disagree

19. I am dissatisfied with my partner's ability to communicate her/his sexual
    desires to me.
    Strongly Agree   1 2 3 4 5 6 7   Strongly Disagree

20. I have no way of knowing when my partner is sexually satisfied.
    Strongly Agree   1 2 3 4 5 6 7   Strongly Disagree

21. I am not satisfied in the majority of our sexual interactions.
    Strongly Agree   1 2 3 4 5 6 7   Strongly Disagree

22. I am pleased with the manner in which mypartner and I communicate with
    each other after sex.
    Strongly Agree   7 6 5 4 3 2 1   Strongly Disagree

Interpretation:

Overall Scores: Add all of the circled items together to arrive at a total score. Scores from 22 - 66 indicate low sexual communication satisfaction; 67 - 110 indicate moderate satisfaction; 111 - 154 indicate high satisfaction.

Satisfaction with YOUR communication: Add your scores on the following items: 1, 3, 5, 6, 8, 9, 11, 14, 16, 17, 21. Scores from 11 - 33 equal low communication satisfaction; 34 - 55 equal moderate satisfaction; 56 - 77 equal high satisfaction.

Satisfaction with PARTNER'S communication: Add your scores on the following items: 2, 10, 13, 15, 18, 19, 20. Scores from 7 - 21 equal low communication satisfaction; 22 - 35 are moderately satisfied; 36 - 49 are highly satisfied.

Discussion: Discussion should surround what accounts for one's willingness or unwillingness to talk about sexual matters. Is sex a social taboo topic? Do we assume that people inherently know how to sexually gratify another? What makes frank sexual discussions uncomfortable? Can you generate communicative ways to initiate such a discussion?

Source: Lawrence R. Wheeless, Virginia Eman Wheeless, and Raymond Baus. "Sexual Communication, Communication Satisfaction, and Solidarity in the Developmental States of Intimate Relationships." The Western Journal of Speech Communication, 48 (1984): 224.

JEALOUSY AND ENVY

Goal: To identify the degree to which you feel and act upon jealousy and envy, and to determine the extent to which it affects your behavior in relationships.

Instructions: Jealousy and envy are interdependent emotions because envy usually stems from jealousy. Jealousy is an intense emotional reaction triggered by fearing the _loss_ of a romantic relationship to a _rival_. Envy is a less intense emotion that stems from the rival's perceived "superior" characteristics that might result in the seduction of one's lover. While jealousy pertains to romantic relationships, envy encompasses general attitudes toward another's material possessions, success, and social and physical attractiveness. Using the following key, place the number in the blank space that most accurately represents your response to the items below: 4 = Frequently; 3 = Sometimes; 2 = Rarely; 1 = Never.

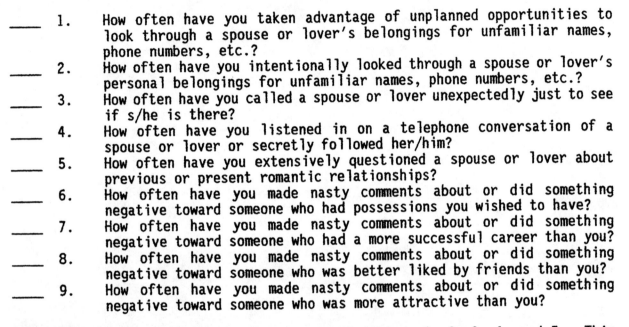

____ 1. How often have you taken advantage of unplanned opportunities to look through a spouse or lover's belongings for unfamiliar names, phone numbers, etc.?

____ 2. How often have you intentionally looked through a spouse or lover's personal belongings for unfamiliar names, phone numbers, etc.?

____ 3. How often have you called a spouse or lover unexpectedly just to see if s/he is there?

____ 4. How often have you listened in on a telephone conversation of a spouse or lover or secretly followed her/him?

____ 5. How often have you extensively questioned a spouse or lover about previous or present romantic relationships?

____ 6. How often have you made nasty comments about or did something negative toward someone who had possessions you wished to have?

____ 7. How often have you made nasty comments about or did something negative toward someone who had a more successful career than you?

____ 8. How often have you made nasty comments about or did something negative toward someone who was better liked by friends than you?

____ 9. How often have you made nasty comments about or did something negative toward someone who was more attractive than you?

Interpretation: Add up your responses to questions 1, 2, 3, 4, and 5. This represents your _jealousy_ score. A score from 4 - 8 indicates low jealousy behavior; 9 - 14 indicates moderate jealousy; 15 - 20 indicates high jealousy. Next, add up your responses to questions 6, 7, 8, and 9. This represents your _envy_ score. A total from 4 - 7 equals low envy behavior; 8 - 12 equals moderate envy behavior; 13 - 16 equals high envy behavior.

Discussion: Persons high in jealousy and envy tend to report having low opinions of themselves, large discrepancies between how they really are and what they would ideally like to be, and value highly such visible achievements as becoming wealthy, famous, well-liked, and, especially, physically attractive. Does this ring true with your experience? Also, low levels of jealousy and envy are normal and can be confronted relatively easily. But high jealousy demands communicative response. As a class, generate ideas about how you can communicatively cope with a jealous partner or friend.

Source: Peter Salovey, and Judith Rodin. "The Heart of Jealousy." _Psychology Today_, September 1985: 22-25, 28-29.

INTERPERSONAL BETRAYAL SCALE

Goal: To identify whether one has violated relationahip expectations, and how one communicatively attempted to repair the damage.

Instructions: A betrayal is a "violation of the trust or expectations on which a relationship is based." As Jones & Burdette (1994, p. 246) note, any long-term relationship is likely to experience such negative experiences, especially when problems occur in relationship expectations, commitment, or trust. To identify your experience with interpersonal betrayal, read each of the following items and respond to them using the scale below:

> 1 = I have never done this
> 2 = I have done this once
> 3 = I have done this a few times
> 4 = I have done this several times
> 5 = I have done this many times

____ 1. Snubbing a friend when with a group you want to impress.
____ 2. Breaking a promise without a good reason.
____ 3. Agreeing with people you really disagree with so that they will accept you.
____ 4. Pretending to like someone you detest.
____ 5. Gossiping about a friend behind his/her back.
____ 6. Making a promise to a friend with no intention of keeping it.
____ 7. Failing to stand up for what you believe in because you want to be accepted by the "in crowd."
____ 8. Complaining to others about your friends or family members.
____ 9. Telling others information given to you in confidence.
____ 10. Lying to a friend.
____ 11. Making a promise to a family member with no intention of keeping it.
____ 12. Failing to stand up for a friend when criticized or belittled by others.
____ 13. Taking family members for granted.
____ 14. Lying to parents/spouse about activities.
____ 15. Wishing that something bad would happen to someone you dislike.

Interpretation: Scores can range from 15 - 75 points. Sum your answers to arrive at your score. In a sample of college students (n = 109), the average score was 35.91. Noncollege adult males (n = 496) scored 35.04 on average, while females (n - 523) averaged 34.96. In a sample of elderly people, age 65 or older, the average score was 27.57.

Discussion: Can betrayals differ from "mild" to "severe?" In other words, what constitutes an act of betrayal for you? And how about for the other in your relationship? How did you discover that you had betrayed another? How did you try to repair the damage? Was it successful? What effect did your betrayal have on the relationship?

Source: Warren H. Jones, and Marsha Parsons Burdette. "Betrayal in Relationships," in Perspectives on Close Relationships, eds Ann L. Weber and John H. Harvey. Boston: Allyn and Bacon, 1994: 251.

DESTRUCTIVE COMMUNICATION PATTERNS
IN RELATIONSHIPS

Goal: The purpose of this exercise is to describe typical communication dialogue that accompanies potentially destructive patterns of communication in relationships.

Instructions: Form groups of 4-6 persons. You will be assigned one of the relationship descriptions below. Construct a <u>relationship context</u> (i.e., husband/wife, father/daughter, boss/employee) and then construct a <u>dialogue</u> of a typical exchange that might occur between these two individuals. Be prepared to role play this dialogue for the class.

1.   <u>Person A</u>: is dominant and certain
         <u>Person B</u>: is submissive and helpful

2.   <u>Person A</u>: is active and indecisive
         <u>Person B</u>: is critical and sends inconsistent messages

3.   <u>Person A</u>: is passive and evasive in conversation
         <u>Person B</u>: is critical and advisory

4.   <u>Person A</u>: is dominant and critical
         <u>Person B</u>: is certain and accepts no responsibility

5.   <u>Person A</u>: is helpful and active
         <u>Person B</u>: is submissive and passive

6.   <u>Person A</u>: is certain and passive
         <u>Person B</u>: is indecisive and shifts topics continuously

Discussion: Discussion should center on which of the six scenarios generates the greatest potential destruction and the least potential destruction. Is it possible to have a healthy relationship if any of these patterns frequently recurs in a relationship? Is one partner more responsible for the destructive potential of the communication pattern than the other person? Do you have any relationships that engage in similar dialogue? How might each scenario be rewritten to make the interaction more constructive?

TERMINATING RELATIONSHIPS

Goal: To identify how you terminate a friendship or intimate relationship, and to identify skills in the communicative resolution of a relationship.

Instructions: Terminating a relationship, particularly a close one, is difficult to do under the best of circumstances. Normally, persons simply avoid one another and thus never have the opportunity to "resolve" the relationship and advance to another one without carrying the baggage of previous relationships. Communicatively ending a relationship, however, is important for the future of both parties. For this exercise, first write a short paragraph about your last relationship that was terminated. What was it like? What was said? What is the current status of your feelings about this relationship? Then form groups of 4-6 persons. Your task is to "reenact" each group members' situation by creating termination dialogue in each of the categories below.

1. **Positive Tone**: Generate dialogue expressing regrets and apologies and hopefully that no hard feelings will result for breaking up.

   _____

   _____

   _____

   _____

2. **Identity Management**: Express reasons for breaking up that relate to your goals--i.e., that life is too short, that you need more independence, that the relationship is not growing.

   _____

   _____

   _____

   _____

3. **Farewell Address**: Figure out how to say "goodbye." Create a message that signals supportiveness for the other, that the relationship was not wasted time, that provides a proper summary of the relationship, and that identifies what your preference is should you run into each other in the future.

   _____

   _____

   _____

   _____

Discussion: Discussion should surround whether you have actually used any of the above three skills for terminating relationships before. Can you envision actually engaging in such dialogue? Why or why not? Given the relationship that was terminated, what do you think might have happened had you attempted to end it communicatively? Why are we reluctant to participate in this form of communication?

COPING WITH RELATIONSHIP LOSS

Goal: This exercise is designed to illuminate how we communicate when a relationship is lost due to break-up or death.

Instructions: One inescapable fact of interpersonal life is that relationships end, whether due to death, unforeseen circumstances, or conscious termination. Theory suggests that when a relationship ends, we must go through a period of "grieving" and/or "account-making." This period of time exists for the purpose of answering "why" questions in order to provide "meaning" for the relationship and its loss.

Situation 1: Relationship Termination: Think of a friendship or intimate relationship that ended. The following are typical communicative ways in which people cope with relationship termination. In the space provided, write down how you behaved in each of these categories.

1. One byproduct of relationship termination is the loss of a couple's "collective" remembering. Provide an example of forgetting your times together. _____
   _____
   _____

2. Relationship loss often generates confusion, misery, loss of control, and the desire to avoid the truth. If you experienced these feelings, provide an example of them. _____
   _____
   _____

3. Disengaged couples usually have discrepant interpretations of their relationship after its break-up. If this occurred, provide an example to illustrate. _____
   _____
   _____

4. Persons often express relationship loss through unaccustomed communicative forms like poetry, music, and writing. Summarize how you expressed the confusion and emotions of your loss through communication. _____
   _____
   _____

5. Persons tend to engage in an "obsessive review" of events in their relationship. Did this happen to you? Explain. _____
   _____
   _____

6. Persons tend to engage in doubts and fantasies about a relationship loss through excessive use of "if onlys." If this happened to you, explain.
   _____
   _____
   _____

Situation 2: Relationship Loss Through Death: Think of someone important to you who has died. Then explain the communicative nature of your grieving process by comparing your behavior with what theory says are common stages of "account-making," or communicative responses to death.

1. Your loss has to be recognized. How did you acknowledge the permanence of death of someone important to you? _____
    _____
    _____

2. Emotions must be released. How did you express your grief emotionally, and what emotions did you express? For how long? _____
    _____
    _____

3. The survivor must develop new skills for living and coping. What changes did you undergo and what skills did you learn as a result of this relationship loss? _____
    _____
    _____

4. The survivor must reinvest emotional energy in new directions. In what way(s) have you done so? _____
    _____
    _____

5. It may take persons a long time to complete "unfinished business" that results from death. Have you completed the grieving process? Have you reconciled with the other's death? _____
    _____
    _____

6. We often use our experiences to create "generativity" or to enlighten others. This occurs primarily through the communicative process of "storytelling." Has this occurred for you? Do you ever have the opportunity to "teach" others through your experiences with relationship loss through death? If so, what do you say? What is the ultimate lesson you have learned from your experiences? _____
    _____
    _____

Discussion: Relationship loss is simultaneously a unique and a common human experience. As a result, we have a need to cope with relationship loss through communication. Classroom discussion, then, should surround identifying common themes that emerge when accounting for the loss of a relationship, and why it is so important to be able to articulate that loss. What are the consequences of a person who does not talk about relationship loss? What should one say to a person who has just terminated an intimate relationship? What should one say to a person who has just loss her/his intimate other through death?

DIAGNOSING YOUR RELATIONSHIP

Goal: To identify your communicative strengths and weaknesses in a specific relationship.

Instructions: Select a relationship that is important to you, i.e., family, friend, or significant love relationship. For each statement below, place a check in the space on the continuum from "rarely" to "often" that best reflects your attitude. Then, in the blank space to the left of each statement, indicate the degree to which you are satisfied with this behavior in your relationship by using the following scale: S = satisfactory, OK = acceptable but not exceptional, D = somewhat disappointing. You may mark an item low on the continuum, but like it that way. Or you may mark an item high, but feel uncomfortable about it. One person's intimacy afterall may be another's anxiety.

Cooperation

_____ 1. We identify, define, and solve our problems together. We respect each other's competence.
Rarely ____ ____ ____ ____ ____ ____ ____ Often

_____ 2. We work together as a team without competing or putting each other down.
Rarely ____ ____ ____ ____ ____ ____ ____ Often

_____ 3. We make decisions together. We make the most of what each of us has to contribute.
Rarely ____ ____ ____ ____ ____ ____ ____ Often

_____ 4. We share our opinions, thoughts, and ideas without becoming argumentative or defensive.
Rarely ____ ____ ____ ____ ____ ____ ____ Often

_____ 5. Overall, I am satisfied with our mutual respect and cooperation in thinking, deciding, and working together.
Rarely ____ ____ ____ ____ ____ ____ ____ Often

Compatibility

_____ 6. We accept and work through our differences to find a common life style with regard to our social and public images.
Rarely ____ ____ ____ ____ ____ ____ ____ Often

_____ 7. We accept and work through our differences to find common values with regard to religion, morality, social concerns, and politics.
Rarely ____ ____ ____ ____ ____ ____ ____ Often

_____ 8. We accept and work through our differences with regard to our social life and choice of friends.
Rarely ____ ____ ____ ____ ____ ____ ____ Often

_____ 9. We accept and work through our differences so that we are able to share a basic approach to roles and rules.
Rarely ____ ____ ____ ____ ____ ____ ____ Often

_____ 10. Overall, I am satisfied with the way we deal with our differences, maintain a life style, and share values.
Rarely _____ _____ _____ _____ _____ _____ _____ Often

Intimacy

_____ 11. We often play together. We put fun into what we do together.
Rarely _____ _____ _____ _____ _____ _____ _____ Often

_____ 12. We express our emotions and feelings openly and freely. We say that we are scared, sad, hurting, angry, or happy.
Rarely _____ _____ _____ _____ _____ _____ _____ Often

_____ 13. We tell each other what we like and dislike. We ask openly for what we want from each other.
Rarely _____ _____ _____ _____ _____ _____ _____ Often

_____ 14. We "let go" with each other. We play, relax, and have fun with each other.
Rarely _____ _____ _____ _____ _____ _____ _____ Often

_____ 15. Overall, I am satisfied with the level of openness and intimacy in our relationship.
Rarely _____ _____ _____ _____ _____ _____ _____ Often

Emotional Support

_____ 16. We listen, understand, and empathize with each other's disappointments, hurts, or problems.
Rarely _____ _____ _____ _____ _____ _____ _____ Often

_____ 17. We encourage and support each other when one of us is making basic life changes or trying new behavior.
Rarely _____ _____ _____ _____ _____ _____ _____ Often

_____ 18. We take responsibility for nurturing when either of us is sick or hurting.
Rarely _____ _____ _____ _____ _____ _____ _____ Often

_____ 19. We are emotionally supportive of each other when either of us feels anxious, dependent, or in need of care.
Rarely _____ _____ _____ _____ _____ _____ _____ Often

_____ 20. Overall, I am satisfied with the nurturing and support we give and receive from each other.
Rarely _____ _____ _____ _____ _____ _____ _____ Often

Discussion: What relationship strengths and weaknesses were you able to identify? What communication skills would you like to work on in this relationship? What have you learned from this diagnosis that can be applied to other important relationships in your life?

Source: Gerald L. Wilson, Alan M. Hantz, and Michael S. Hanna. "Diagnosing Your Relationship," in Interpersonal Growth Through Communication. Dubuque, Iowa: William C. Brown, 1989, pp. 305-306.

QUALITY INTERPERSONAL COMMUNICATION

Quality interpersonal communication in relationships tends to be characterized by the following (this is what "ought" to underlie the communication found in a good relationship).

1. **Empathy**: the ability to accurately understand another individual; identifying her/his feelings, attitudes, etc.

2. **Equality**: mutual respect for each other; no one is superior or inferior to the other.

3. **Openness**: not hiding true thoughts and feelings; to allow the potential for relationships to grow.

4. **Supportiveness**: genuine concern for the other; helping the other to meet his/her needs and potentials.

5. **Positiveness**: a general good or "up" feeling toward the relationship; positive regard and feeling of warmth toward another.

6. **Spontaneity**: interaction that accurately reflects the immediate and genuine reactions of the participants to one another (opposite: cautious, inhibited, preplanned).

7. **Here and Now**: it is best to deal with present feelings rather than always dragging up past issues.

8. **Authenticity**: willingness to acknowledge our own ideas, thoughts, feelings, and to communicate them when appropriate, frankly, and without distortion (leveling = a congruency of feelings with expressions of feelings).

9. **Acceptance**: to genuinely accept another as that person is.

10. **Trust**: essential ingredient; can be sense of character, good will, personal attraction, or any of numerous factors; also, absence of fear that the other will do something against your welfare.

IMPROVING COMMUNICATION IN
RELATIONSHIPS

Goal: This handout is a potpourri of ideas and suggestions for improving communication in relationships. It is designed to synthesize information on communication skills. It is necessarily incomplete, but potentially useful.

A. **Intrapersonal Improvements**

   1. Know your level of commitment to the relationship.

   2. Accept responsibility in the relationship.

   3. Attempt to express your opinions and feelings.

   4. Attempt to be openminded and not too constraining in the relationship.

   5. Work on constructive criticism of self, other, and the relationship. Don't avoid problems, but be careful of only using negative judgments. For example, "if I accept your perception or solution, what might be the consequences or implications for me and the relationship?" Or "I'd like some feedback on my idea about us."

   6. Be honest.

B. **Interpersonal Improvements**--Remember that a relationship is a system; therefore, any change by you, the other, or both will cause reverberations in the whole system.

   1. **Analyze Your Needs**--self knowledge. If you clarify your needs and goals, often, then, you can get what you want.

   2. **Check Your Perceptions**--check the meanings you attach to others and yourself. Watch stereotypes and categorized perceptual sets (perceptual sets, however, are ways to let you organize information). Check your categories against those of others.

      a. Identify your perceptual sets; don't let them get too rigid.
      b. Seek out other perceptions; all perceptions are only partial views.
      c. Get perceptions of other persons (people have reasons for things and behaviors).
      d. Internalize the premise of uniqueness; no two people are alike.
      e. Be aware that you can change your perceptions by changing your behavior and vice versa.

   3. **Confirm the Other**--transact appropriately, confirm the needs of others. Tangential feedback is where you don't allow the other the pleasure of being understood. Ask yourself: do I tend to engage in behaviors that confirm the other person's uniqueness or that increase her/his sense of self-worth?

134

4. Use Active Verbal and Nonverbal Participation--if you don't put energy into the relationship, the relationship will quickly cease to exist. Active participation breeds trust, accuracy, knowledge, familiarity, etc.

5. Communication Skills--be concerned with the process of communication; look at how things are occurring not just what is happening.

C. Relationship Improvements

1. Analyze the Relationship--realize that relationships change, relationships require attention, and relationships progress gradually and sequentially.

2. The Good Relationship--the good relationship is one that serves the functions for which it was formed. Know the reasons for the existence of the relationship and know the goals of each party-- i.e., what does each person want out of the relationship? Realize that goals do change.

3. Relationship Rules--rules in relationships prescribe boundaries and govern behavior. All relationships prescribe boundaries, hence, they all have rules. Know what they are and what subjects, behaviors, etc., are acceptable or not, need changing or not. For example, punctuality and not talking back may be relational rules. If rules need to be established or changed, take the risk to talk about the relationship itself.

4. Rationality--don't arbitrarily buy into the concept of rationality. It is not always logic that is best, nor is it true that people are inherently rational; in fact, people tend to be nonrational in the way they cope with their relationships.

5. Content and Relational Levels of Communication
    a. Be aware that both levels exist; and be aware that the tendency is to talk only about the content level.
    b. If a content disagreement starts a relational disagreement, then meta-communicate: "what gives you the idea that I don't want to listen to you?"
    c. Nonverbal signals may be good clues to the relational level: eye contact, inflection of voice, questioning like "you don't really think . . ."

6. Self-Disclosure

    a. Be clear on the level of involvement and intimacy in relationships and the corresponding level of self-disclosure. Know that self-disclosure is both a reason for the level of intimacy and a way to create intimacy.
    b. Make sure the situation is appropriate for self-disclosure, but also be willing to take risks to self-disclose.
    c. Realize that what is self-disclosure for one may not be for another. Look for verbal and nonverbal clues for clarification.

135

d.   Try initiating self-disclosure sometimes rather than always responding to another's self-disclosure so as to eliminate risk.

7.   <u>Listening</u>

a.   Actively listen; request clarification of other's positions; restate or paraphrase and request clarification for accuracy. For example, "what I hear you saying is . . ." or "Is this correct?"
b.   Watch for interruptions because they signify nonlistening.
c.   Observe the flow of discussion. Does one comment logically follow the other?
d.   You might set procedures so both can be assured time to voice opinions, concerns, etc. This would make listening easier.
e.   Look beyond what is said--the words--to see the feelings and issues occurring relationally.

8.   <u>Conflict</u>

a.   Be aware of yours and the culture's assumptions about conflict.
b.   Try to make it acceptable for conflict to occur; remember that conflicts do have positive benefits.
c.   Look at the conflict in terms of win/lose, win/win, or lose/lose as well as in terms of concern for self, other, or both. Now, is this really what you would like to happen?
d.   Be creative with the process of conflict. For example, have each individual take on the other's role in order to see how each is perceiving the other's position.
e.   Emphasize areas of agreement rather than areas of disagreement to help manage conflicts.

9.   <u>The Way We Were Syndrome</u>--Be aware that some dyads just are not satisfying regardless. Recognize that no solution--only a parting of the dyad--is possible.

Answers to Perception Quiz:

1 = bottom
2 = right to left
3 = right
4 = yellow, gold, red, white, black
5 = Q & Z
6 = 1 & 0 (operator)
7 = right w/left
8 = 20
9 = red
10 = 88
11 = 5
12 = top left to bottom left
13 = 12 (not UHF)
14 = right
15 = top
16 = clockwise
17 = F. D. Roosevelt
18 = 8
19 = left
20 = 5
21 = 6
22 = bashful
23 = 8
24 = free
25 = ace of spades
26 = left
27 = "one"
28 = * and #
29 = 3
30 = counterclockwise

Answers to Marriage Quiz: Items 2, 5, 6, 12, and 16 are true; all other items are false.

Listening Exercise: The Farm Story: After graduation from college, Carl Franz returned to his parent's farm and they formed a partnership. After one year, they decide that the 240 acres which they own and farm are not enough to make a profitable return for the three of them. Furthermore, they feel that with their present equipment, they could easily farm additional land. They decide to try to buy an additional 60 acres. The 420 acre farm adjoining theirs on the sough and east is owned by a local bank, and it is from this farm that the Franz's want to make their purchase.

Acknowledgements

Janis F. Anderson, Peter A. Anderson and Arthur D. Jansen, "The Measurement of Nonverbal Immediacy" from the Journal of Applied Communication Research, pp. 174-175. Copyright © by Speech Communication Association. Reprinted by permission of the publisher.

Marquita L. Byrd, The Intracultural Communication Book, pp. 192-197. Copyright © 1993 by McGraw-Hill, Inc. Reprinted by permission of the publisher.

Gail Armstead Hankins, "Don't Judge a Book by its Cover" from The Speech Teacher, Summer, 5, #4, pp. 8. Copyright © 1991 by Speech Communication Association. Reprinted by permission of the publisher.

Ken Hawkinson, "Two Exercises on Diversity and Gender" from The Speech Communication Teacher, Vol. 8, #1 Fall. Copyright © 1993 by Speech Communication Association. Reprinted by permission of the publisher.

Michael L. Hecht, "The Conceptualization and Measurement of Interpersonal Communications Satisfaction" from Human Communication Research, 4, #3, pp. 253-264. Copyright © 1978 by Sage Publications, Inc. Reprinted by permission of the publisher.

C. Hendrick and S. Hendrick, "A Relationship-Specific of the Love Attitudes Scale" from Handbook of Replication in the Behavioral and Social Sciences, J. W. Newliep, ed., Vol. 5, #4, pp. 239-254. Copyright © 1990 by Select Press, Corte Madera, CA.

D. A. Infante and A. S. Rancer, from "A Conceptualization and Measure of Arguementativeness" in the Journal of Personality Assessment, Vol. 46, pp. 76. Copyright © 1982 by Lawrence Erlbaum Associates. Reprinted by permission of the publisher.

D. A. Infante and C. J. Wigley, from "Verbal Aggressiveness: An Interpersonal Model and Measure" in Communication Monographs, Vol. 53, pp. 64. Copyright © 1986 by Speech Communication Association. Reprinted by permission of the publisher.

Linda A. Joesting, Communication Research Associates, from Communicate! A Workbook For Interpersonal Communication, 4th Edition, pp. 88-89, 183-186, 314. Copyright © 1990 by Communication Research Association. Reprinted by permission of Kendall/Hunt Publishing Company, Dubuque, IA.

Warren H. Jones and Marsha Parsons Burdette, "Betrayal in Relationships" from Perspectives on Close Relationships, Eds. Ann L Weber and John H. Harvey, pp. 251. Copyright © 1994 by Allyn and Bacon. Reprinted by permission of the publisher.

Sidney M. Jourard, Self-Disclosure: An Experimental Analysis of the Transparent Self, pp. 189-191. Copyright © 1979 by Robert E. Krieger Publishing Co. Reprinted by permission of John Wiley & Sons, Inc.